Who Am I?

*Pre-School/Kindergarten
Teacher's Manual*

Mary Jo Smith

Jerelyn Helmberger

Theological Advisors
Rev. Richard M. Hogan
Rev. John M. LeVoir

IMAGE OF GOD SERIES

Image of God, Inc., Brooklyn Center, MN 55430
Ignatius Press, San Francisco

Nihil obstat: David A. Dillon, S.T.D.

Imprimatur: ✠ John R. Roach, D.D.
                  Archbishop of St. Paul and Minneapolis
                  August 15, 1986

Cover illustration by Barbara Harasyn

Second Edition
Published 1993 by Ignatius Press, San Francisco
© 1986 Image of God, Inc.
All rights reserved
ISBN 0–89870–321–2
Printed in Hong Kong

ACKNOWLEDGMENTS
We wish to express our gratitude to all those who helped make this work possible. To our husbands, Jim Smith and Gary Helmberger, for their support, understanding, and encouragement. To our children and families, who helped in so many intangible ways while this program was being written.

We are grateful also to Monsignor Stanley J. Srnec for his encouragement and for allowing us to pilot this program at the parish of St. Raphael. Further, we wish to thank the St. Raphael Sunday School teachers and aides for using and reviewing this program in the 1985–86 school year.

A special thanks to Terry Skiba and to Mary Sandstrom for reading, contributing to, and supporting this program.

Lastly, we wish to thank Rev. Richard M. Hogan and Rev. John M. LeVoir for teaching us the application of Pope John Paul II's new synthesis, which is the basis for this program. Through their guidance, support, editing, and encouragement, this program became a reality.

                                        Mary Jo Smith
                                        Jerelyn Helmberger

Contents

About the Image of God Series

As might be expected from the title, the Image of God religion series has as its foundation the creation of man in God's own image and likeness. Human beings are persons because they are like God, made in God's own image. This is an objective truth that is at the same time central to man's experience. Every human being knows that he or she is different from the animals and the plants. This is at the heart of his or her subjective experience. The reason human beings are different is revealed in the objective order, but it explains the subjective experience of every human being. At one and the same time, the truth that man is created in the image of God is both objective and subjective. For, if human beings are in God's image, then their only hope, if they are to be true to their very selves, is to function as God does! God's revelation of Himself, especially that shown to human beings by the Incarnation, thus becomes crucial if they are to be true to their own selves.

Human persons are not only in the image of God, but God is in the image of human beings.* Thus, the study of man reveals truths about God, and the study of God reveals truths about man. It is on the basis of this double movement that the Image of God series employs experience to teach the truths of the Faith. For example, human beings are like God because they are persons. They are different from God because they have bodies. The love uniting the members of a family in a communion of persons should reflect the perfect love of the trinitarian communion of Persons. Experience is used to illustrate how we are like God and sometimes how we are different from God. It is never used to "govern" or define truths of the Faith. Thus, in the Image of God series, there can be found two fundamental progressions: one beginning with man and moving to God, and the other beginning with God and moving to man. Obviously, the study of Christ, the God-man, is at the center of both these movements because it is only in Christ, the perfect Image of God, that the true meaning of our experience, as human images of God, is revealed.

The Image of God series is centered on the subjective emphasis found in the writings of Pope John Paul II. The Pope is an extraordinary person! Born in Poland shortly after the First World War, Karol Wojtyla lived and suffered through both the Nazi scourge and the Communist domination of his beloved homeland. Both the Nazis and the Communists showed scant respect for human rights. The youthful Wojtyla's experiences under their tyranny had a profound effect on him. He began to understand that the only defense against the outrages of ideologies such as these was a vehement insistence on the inherent dignity of each and every human person.

* See Pope John Paul II, "Faith Culminates in the Truth That God Is Love", *L'Osservatore Romano*, English edition, vol. 18, no. 40, October 7, 1985, p. 1, where John Paul teaches that "Seeing that man is created in the image and likeness of God, there is reason for speaking of God 'in the image and likeness of man' ".

While John Paul's interest in the dignity and rights of the individual human person may have been spurred initially by his own tragic experiences in Poland, it was nourished and enriched through his studies. Even before he entered the underground seminary, he was well acquainted with the Gospel and had an active prayer life. He found in the activity of God, as revealed in the Sacred Scriptures, an affirmation of man's dignity. After all, God had made human beings in His image. Further, God so loved the world that He sent His only Son. There can be no greater confirmation of the dignity of each and every human being than the Incarnation.

After his ordination in 1946, Father Karol Wojtyla was sent to Rome to study. He took his doctorate in mystical theology. Returning to Poland on the completion of his doctorate in theology, the young priest was soon assigned to the University of Lublin/Cracow, where he began a second doctorate in philosophy. The Lublin/Cracow philosophers were phenomenological realists. Because Father Wojtyla was earning a doctorate under their guidance, he studied phenomenology. Phenomenology begins its investigation of reality with human experience—it begins with the human subject. Given this emphasis on the dignity of the individual human person, Father Wojtyla discovered in the philosophical system—with its extraordinary emphasis on the individual—a vehicle marvelously suited for communicating the truth of human dignity to the world. He saw that phenomenology was not only an excellent tool for presenting his central insight about human persons, but that it was also most practical because it was most effective. Karol Wojtyla recognized that in some way phenomenology captures the attention of modern man. It speaks to the people of our age with a conviction and force that even the system of Saint Thomas Aquinas cannot approach.

Even if Father Karol Wojtyla had never been chosen for the papal office, his work would have represented a new and original milestone in man's reflection on himself and the Gospel. Pope John Paul II's philosophical insights, when applied to the truths of the Faith, produce a new theological synthesis founded on a new and revealing "subjective turn". The unifying element in this synthesis is the individual subject—the human person—created by God in His own image and redeemed by the God-man. Can it not be suggested that such a synthesis is comparable to the previous syntheses of Saint Augustine and Saint Thomas Aquinas?

Bishop Karol Wojtyla is the first Pope who as a bishop participated in all the sessions of the Second Vatican Council. Through Wojtyla and the other Polish bishops, a new Christian synthesis of the Faith and reason (developed in Poland at the University of Lublin/Cracow) was received into the conciliar documents. John Paul II is teaching the world the fruits of this new presentation of the Faith, which is found in the documents of the Council. However, it is unfortunate that the papal theology has been largely ignored. Still, there are some bright spots. One of those bright spots is the new Image of God religion series. The new presentation of the Faith, taught to the world through John Paul II, is the basis for the Image of God religion series, including, of course, the pre-school/kindergarten program. This program, written for a new generation of Catholics, is as exciting as the John Paul II papacy!

The Image of God series is founded on seven key ideas: God, Creation, Christ, Church, Grace, Sacraments, and Commandments. Each one of these seven key, but rather familiar, ideas is taught from the new subjective viewpoint found in the conciliar documents and in the writings of Pope John Paul II.

The pre-school/kindergarten program has as its emphasis the two key ideas already discussed above: God and Creation (image of God). Consequently, the material in each lesson is presented in the light of the truth of our creation by God in His image and likeness. This truth is the common thread uniting the pre-school/kindergarten program. It is one of several uniting the entire Image of God series.

In the new synthesis of the Faith present in the Image of God series, there is a new unity between the creation and the Redemption. God the Son, the perfect Image of the Father, became a man, Jesus Christ, to show us who we are and how we are to act. Because we are made in the image of God, we cannot know ourselves unless we know God. Even without original sin and the Fall, we would have needed to know God if we were to know ourselves. Christ, the God-man, reveals God as Love, especially through the Cross and Resurrection. In revealing God, Christ showed us who we are and how to act. Thus, Christ fulfills creation by revealing man to himself.* Creation (and, in particular, man—pinnacle of creation) finds fulfillment in Christ the Redeemer, and Christ the Redeemer completes creation.

In tune with the subjective emphasis of the new synthesis, the Image of God series presents the commandments in a new way. The commandments are part and parcel of God's self-revelation. The commandments were given by God to Moses on Mount Sinai as is recorded in the Old Testament. Because the Old Testament is a preparation for Christ and because Christ reveals man to himself, the Old Testament is a gradual revelation of man to himself. First and foremost among the revelations in the Old Testament are the commandments. They are directions God gives us so we can act as Christ acted. In other words, they teach us how to love, because God's acts are always acts of love. Of course, we are free to reject the commandments, just as we are free to reject Christ. However, when we do not follow the commandments and Christ, we fail to act as the beings we are: images of God. We sin. We hurt ourselves, because to be human means to act as God acts. Sin is like a self-inflicted wound. It hurts us, and it also offends God. It is to act in a non-human (non-image of God) way. The commandments are not so much laws or rules imposed from the outside on us. Rather, they are more like blueprints of our existence. We are free not to follow the revelation of who we are, but then we destroy ourselves. God is not telling us "You must do these things" so much as He is telling us "My commandments show you how I made you. Don't destroy yourselves by deviating from them."

In John Paul II's new synthesis, the Church is the mystical person of Christ. The Church is not a thing or an object, but a person. It

---

* See the Second Vatican Council's *Gaudium et Spes, The Pastoral Constitution on the Church in the Modern World*, no. 22.

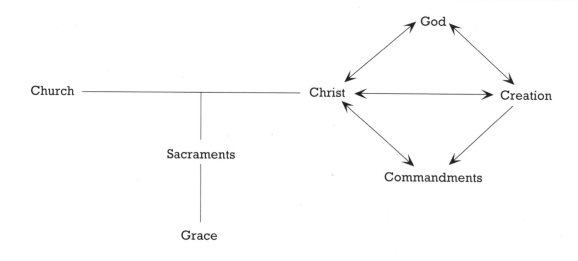

Diagram Explanation

Human persons are made in the image of God. Further, God can be said to be in the image of human beings. Christ, the perfect Image of the Father, is sent by the Father and returns to Him. Creation, the first revelation of God, is incomplete. It looks to Christ Who reveals God more fully. Christ fulfills creation by revealing man to himself and restoring human beings to the possibility of acting as images of God. The Church is the mystical person of Christ continuing Christ's mission. The sacraments are the very "touch" of Christ, which gives grace, God's life. This divine life makes it possible for human beings to live as images of God and to share eternity with God. With grace, it is possible again for the human body to express the human person. The commandments, given by God in the Old Testament and fulfilled in Christ, teach human beings how to act as images of God.

is one mystical person, Christ, formed through a union of persons: Christ and all the baptized. This union is accomplished by the Holy Spirit through the gift of grace. As a person, the Church possesses a mind and a will, that is, the mind and the will of Christ. Christ carries on His mission and His work in the world today through the Church, His mystical person.

In the Image of God religion series, the sacraments are presented as the physical acts of Christ (Church) today. Just as Christ possessed a body through His human nature, so His mystical person, the Church, has a physical aspect. The sacraments are the most important physical acts of the body of the Church. They manifest, or express, the person of the Church, that is, Christ. When we celebrate a sacrament, Christ "touches us" in a way similar to His "touch" two thousand years ago.

At the same time, the sacraments give grace, God's life. Since God created Adam and Eve to share His life on earth and to live with Him forever in heaven, Adam and Eve had grace, because grace is necessary if one is to be with God in heaven. However, Adam and Eve lost God's life when they sinned. They also hurt themselves, so that it was almost impossible for them to act as images of God. Their minds and wills no longer governed their bodies. The human body no longer expressed the human person properly. To be human is to act like an image of God in and through a body. After original sin, this was almost impossible.

Therefore, after original sin human beings were not fully human. Human beings could not share God's life on earth or go to heaven (because they had lost grace), and they could not even act as images of God. Christ, God the Son, came and showed us who we are and how to act. (This we would have needed even without original sin.) But He also restored grace. In the new presentation of the Faith, grace has three important functions for those living after original sin. It unites us with God here on earth; it makes it possible for us to live with God forever in heaven; and it enables us to think and to choose as human beings, as images of God, again. With grace, we can understand what Christ revealed, and we can act as

He did. Grace does not always make it easy to act as we should, but it makes it possible for the mind and will to govern the body, that is, for the human body to express the human person.

The entire Image of God series, and this pre-school/kindergarten program in particular, is founded on the Holy Scriptures. The Scriptures, together with Tradition, contain all that God intended to reveal about Himself, us, and the world. This Revelation is the object of the Church's Faith. The Image of God series uses seven key ideas as the organizing principles of the Catholic Faith, that is, of all that God revealed about Himself in Tradition and Scripture. Clearly, Scripture, together with Tradition, will pervade each of the seven key areas. However, Scripture and Tradition not only contain the Faith, they are also, in their own way, objects of faith. After all, we do believe not only that God revealed Himself, but that He revealed Himself through Scripture and Tradition. As objects of faith, the Scriptures and Tradition are examined within the context of the Church, one of the seven key ideas. As the living, mystical Christ, the Church is the legitimate interpreter of Revelation, that is, of the Scriptures and of Tradition. Because Christ is the perfect and complete Revelation of the Father, He is the legitimate interpreter of all Revelation before Him, that is, the Old Testament, and He is the legitimate interpreter of all that is about Him, that is, the New Testament. As the mystical Christ today, the Church carries on the task of interpreting Scripture and Tradition. As objects of faith, Scripture and Tradition are seen in the Image of God series in the context of the Church.

Each of the seven ideas is studied every year in the Image of God series. However, each year emphasizes two or three of these ideas and treats them more extensively. As noted in Outline 1, each of the seven topic areas is emphasized in one of the four primary grades, pre-school/kindergarten through grade three. Similarly, each idea is emphasized in one of the intermediate years, grades four through six. In the two junior high years, grades seven and eight, each topic area finds an emphasis. After the foundation is laid in the primary years, the intermediate and junior high years expand on each topic area and explain it in greater depth according to the development of the child.

Pope John Paul II's new presentation of the Faith is founded on the cornerstone of the creation of human beings in the image and likeness of God. In other words, it is founded on the incomparable dignity and value of each and every human being. It presents the Faith as the hope for all people everywhere. There could hardly be a message more important for the twentieth century to hear. Our century has seen millions of men and women killed in war and in concentration camps; millions of homeless and abandoned refugees driven from their lands; countless millions of unborn children killed in their mothers' wombs; women, children, and even men treated as sex objects for the use of others; and workers treated worse than machines—their lives being measured by their usefulness. Our century desperately needs to hear about the value and dignity of every human person as confirmed by the Gospel. It is this message of hope that the Image of God series tries to convey to the children and young adults who use it.

The Seven Basic Topics
God
Creation
Christ
Church
Grace
Sacraments
Commandments

Topics Emphasized in Each Grade Level
Pre-school & Kindergarten
God
Creation
Grade 1
Grace
Sacraments
Grade 2
Sacraments
Commandments
Grade 3
Christ
Church
Grade 4
God
Grace
Commandments
Grade 5
Christ
Church
Sacraments
Grade 6
Old Testament—Creation
Grade 7
God
Creation
Christ
Commandments
Grade 8
Church
Grace
Sacraments
Grade 9
Review of the seven topics
Grade 10
Sacred Scripture
Grade 11
History of the Church
Grade 12
Communion of Persons

Perhaps if enough children and young people recognize their own value and worth, calamities such as our century has suffered will not befall future generations.

—Rev. Richard M. Hogan

Introduction

The Who Am I? *Program*

The *Who Am I?* program is a Catholic religion curriculum for children from three years old to kindergarten age. This program is centered on a new approach found in the writings and teachings of Pope John Paul II. This approach stresses the dignity of each individual as a person made in the image of God. The *Who Am I?* program has as its emphasis two key truths of the Faith: God and creation. These key truths form the unifying element of the lessons. The material in each lesson revolves around fundamentals of our Faith stated in terms the children can understand and remember.

This program was designed to be used in any of the following three settings: Sunday school, five-day pre-school, or kindergarten. How to use the *Who Am I?* program in each specific setting is discussed on subsequent pages of this teacher's manual.

The *Who Am I?* program consists of the following material: a combined pre-school/kindergarten teacher's manual, a pattern packet for the teachers, and children's workbooks—two workbooks for pre-school-age children and one for kindergarten children.

The combined pre-school/kindergarten teacher's manual consists of 17 basic lessons with four kindergarten extensions. In addition, there are nine basic liturgical and holiday lessons with two kindergarten extensions. In its entirety, this program contains 32 separate lessons. The content of each lesson is discussed in directions for the specific settings.

The pattern packet contains 25 patterns. These patterns will aid you in preparing the various art and craft projects suggested in the lessons. Depending on the age and skill level of the children, you may choose to cut cardboard tracers from the patterns and allow each child to trace and cut the project pieces themselves, or you may cut all the project pieces from the patterns.

The workbooks contain worksheets that relate either to the stories suggested in the lesson or to the Lesson Focus. You can send the worksheets home to be completed, or you may prefer that the students complete them in the classroom and then take them home. In either case, these worksheets should be used as take-home material, because they furnish the basis for parent–child faith discussions.

The materials of the *Who Am I?* program form an integrated whole, and it is the hope of the authors that these materials will aid catechists in bringing the Good News of Jesus Christ to the little children.

Using Who Am I? *in a Sunday School Setting*

This teacher's manual contains 17 lessons. In addition, there are nine basic liturgical and holiday lessons. There are six kindergarten extensions included in this manual. You, as the pre-school teacher, may wish to include some of the material in these extensions in your curriculum. However, these extensions are designed specifically for children of kindergarten age. (Worksheets for these extensions are found only in the kindergarten workbook.) These kindergarten extensions are not part of the pre-school program. The pre-school program includes a total of 26 lessons. Each lesson is made up of five components: Lesson Focus, Concepts of Faith, Lesson Presentation, Living the Lesson, and Extending the Lesson.

The *Lesson Focus* gives you, the teacher, an insight to the emphasis of the lesson. The Lesson Focus, along with the *Concepts of Faith*, defines the lesson within Pope John Paul II's new synthesis. We suggest that you read the Lesson Focus and the Concepts of Faith before class. These two sections provide the necessary background for the Lesson Presentation. The vocabulary words that are key to each lesson are highlighted. Definitions of these words are given for the children.

The *Lesson Presentation* consists of two parts, the Application with discussion questions and the Suggested Stories, included in most of the lessons. (In the few lessons without stories, other activities are recommended.) The Application is a presentation of the lesson using suggested props that stimulate the children visually. Every attempt has been made to suggest readily available materials for these props. Discussion questions follow the Application, giving the children an opportunity to verbalize what they have learned. There are usually two Suggested Stories (A and B) for each lesson. Only one story need be used. (If your Sunday school enrolls three- and four-year-olds, we suggest that the three-year-olds use story A, and the four-year-olds use story B. Another option is to use the A stories for all ages the first year and the B stories for the second year.) The stories also include review questions to help the children restate the story in their own words, increasing their retention.

The workbooks for the pre-school children include worksheets that relate to the Suggested Stories or the Lesson Focus. We suggest that if Story A is read, the corresponding A worksheets (usually two per lesson) be used. Of course, if story B is read, then the B worksheets should be used. These worksheets provide activities for the children, such as coloring, cutting, dot to dot, matching. These worksheets add another stimulus for retention of the lesson theme, and the worksheets aid the children in developing some of the basic skills they will need when they enter school. These worksheets can be given to the children who finish the art and craft project before the rest of the class, or the worksheets can be used to expand the class, should there be additional time. In any case, the worksheets should be sent home, because they furnish the basis for parent–child faith discussions.

The *Living the Lesson* section offers the children an opportunity to apply the theme of the lesson in their daily lives. The question–answer format stimulates practical discussion. The answers suggested in the teacher's manual are not necessarily the answers the children will give, but it is hoped that you, the teacher, will be able to lead the discussion toward these or similar answers.

The *Extending the Lesson* section includes as many as three art and craft projects. You may choose to make any one of these projects. The materials needed for each project are listed separately. For some of these art projects, patterns are provided in the supplementary packet included with this teacher's manual. Each project directly relates to either the focus of the lesson or to one of the suggested stories. By working with their hands on these projects, the children are better able to retain the lesson concept. The action rhymes included in this section are a change of pace to be used during the class period to accommodate the children's short attention spans. Each lesson should begin and conclude with prayer. The use of the formal prayers of the Church—the "Our Father", the "Hail Mary", and the "Glory Be"—is strongly encouraged. We have included short prayers written in the words of children. We hope that this format will encourage your students to offer their own spontaneous prayers along with the use of formal prayer.

The following is a suggested time breakdown for the Sunday school classroom. Obviously, when you work with pre-school children, time cannot be rigidly structured. You will probably want to adjust this model to fit your specific classroom.

    A. Welcoming children, sharing, and opening prayer (5 minutes)
    B. Lesson presentation (10 minutes)
    C. Action rhyme and songs (physical activity) (5 minutes)
    D. Suggested story and review questions (10–15 minutes)
    E. Art project (10 minutes)
    F. Living the lesson (10 minutes)
    G. Closing prayer (5 minutes)

Using Who Am I? in a Pre-School Setting

This teacher's manual contains 17 lessons. In addition, there are nine basic liturgical and holiday lessons. There are six kindergarten extensions included in this manual. You, as the pre-school teacher, may wish to include some of the material in these extensions in your curriculum. However, these extensions are designed specifically for children of kindergarten age. (Worksheets for these extensions are found only in the kindergarten workbook.) These kindergarten extensions are not part of the pre-school program. The pre-school program includes a total of 26 lessons. Each lesson is made up of five components: Lesson Focus, Concepts of Faith, Lesson Presentation, Living the Lesson, and Extending the Lesson.

The *Lesson Focus* gives you, the teacher, an insight to the emphasis of the lesson. The Lesson Focus, along with the *Concepts of Faith*, defines the lesson within Pope John Paul II's new synthesis. We suggest that you read the Lesson Focus and the Concepts of Faith before class. These two sections provide the necessary background for the Lesson Presentation. The vocabulary words that are key to each lesson are highlighted. Definitions of these words are given for the children.

The *Lesson Presentation* consists of two parts, the Application with discussion questions and the Suggested Stories, included in most of the lessons. (In the few lessons without stories, other activities are recommended.) The Application is a presentation of the lesson using suggested props that stimulate the children visually. Every attempt has been made to suggest readily available materials for these props. Discussion questions follow the Application, giving the children an opportunity to verbalize what they have learned. They could be used as the conclusion to this first class period or as a review for the next period. There are usually two Suggested Stories (A and B) for each lesson. In the second class period, one of the suggested stories can be read. The second story, included with most of the lessons, can be used in a subsequent class period to expand on the lesson. The stories also include review questions to help the children restate the story in their own words, increasing their retention.

The workbook for pre-school children includes worksheets (usually four) that relate to the Suggested Stories or the Lesson Focus. The A worksheets can be used after reading the A Suggested Story and the B worksheets after the B story. These worksheets provide activities for the children, such as coloring, cutting, dot to dot, and matching. These worksheets add another stimulus for retention of the lesson theme and aid in developing some of the basic skills the children will need when they enter school. The worksheets can be used in a class period to review the story and the Lesson Focus. The worksheets should be sent home with the children, because they furnish the basis for parent–child faith discussions.

We suggest that the *Living the Lesson* section be used in the fourth class period. The question–answer format of this fourth day stimulates practical discussion. It offers the children an opportunity to apply the theme of the lesson in their daily lives. The answers suggested in the teacher's manual are not necessarily the answers the children will give, but we hope that you will be able to lead the discussion toward these or similar answers.

On the fifth day you can choose from one of the art and craft projects suggested in the *Extending the Lesson* section. The materials needed for each project are listed separately. For some of these art projects, patterns are provided in the supplementary packet included with this teacher's manual. Each project directly relates to either the focus of the lesson or to one of the suggested stories. By working with their hands on these projects, the children are better able to retain the lesson concept. Included in this section is an action rhyme. This rhyme can be used during any of the class periods as a change of pace and to help channel the children's energies. Each class period should begin and conclude with prayer. The use of the formal prayers of the Church—the "Our Father", the "Hail Mary", and the "Glory Be"—is strongly encouraged. We have included short prayers written in the words of children. It is hoped that this format will encourage your students to offer their own spontaneous prayers along with the use of formal prayer.

Every attempt has been made to provide enough material in the lessons to fill four or five twenty- to thirty-minute class periods. In each lesson, the children are stimulated in a variety of ways to increase their retention of the lesson.

The following is a suggested schedule for pre-school. Obviously, when you work with pre-school children, time cannot be rigidly structured. You will want to adjust this model to fit your specific needs.

Day 1. Application and Discussion Questions
Day 2. Suggested Story and Review Questions
Day 3. Suggested Story and Review Questions
Day 4. Living the Lesson
Day 5. Art and Craft Project

Expansion Material includes worksheets, additional art and craft projects, and action rhymes.

Using Who Am I? in a Kindergarten Setting

This teacher's manual includes 17 basic lessons with four kindergarten extensions: 6K, Church Leaders; 10K, Mass; 13K, Jesus, Our Example; and 14K, The Rosary. In addition, there are nine basic liturgical and holiday lessons with two kindergarten extensions: 18K, All Saints' Day; and 25K, the Stations of the Cross. The kindergarten program includes a total of 32 lessons. Each lesson is made up of five components: Lesson Focus, Concepts of Faith, Lesson Presentation, Living the Lesson, and Extending the Lesson.

The *Lesson Focus* gives you an insight into the emphasis of the lesson. The *Lesson Focus*, along with the *Concepts of Faith*, defines the lesson within Pope John Paul II's new synthesis. The vocabulary words that are key to each lesson are highlighted. Definitions of these words are given for the children. The vocabulary words can be an introduction to the lesson. You may want to write the vocabulary words on the blackboard letter by letter, having the children identify each letter. When the entire word is written, the children can be led to sound out the word.

The *Concepts of Faith* is a question–answer format that restates the definitions of the vocabulary words. This question–answer format can be used together with the vocabulary words to introduce the lesson on the first day.

The *Lesson Presentation* consists of two parts, the Application with discussion questions and the Suggested Stories, included in most of the lessons. (In the few lessons without stories, other activities are recommended.) The Application may be taught in the second class period, with the story or stories following on the next day. The Application is a presentation of the lesson using suggested props that stimulate the children visually. Every attempt has been made to suggest readily available materials for these props. The Application is followed by discussion questions. These questions give the children an opportunity to verbalize what they have learned. The discussion questions could be used as the conclusion to the second class period or as a review for the next period. In the third class period, one of the Suggested Stories can be read. The second story, included with most of the lessons, can either be omitted or used in a subsequent class period to expand on the lesson. The stories also include review questions to help the children restate the story in their own words, increasing their retention.

The workbook for kindergarten children includes worksheets (usually three) that relate to the Suggested Stories or the Lesson Focus. These worksheets provide activities for the children, such as matching, tracing letters, and recognition of numbers, of letters, and of shapes and sizes. These worksheets add another stimulus for retention of the lesson theme, and they aid the children in mastering some of the basic skills taught in kindergarten. These worksheets can be used during any of the class periods after the Application. The worksheets should be sent home with the children, because they furnish the basis for parent–child faith discussions.

We suggest that the *Living the Lesson* section be used in the fourth class period. The question–answer format of this fourth day stimulates practical discussion. It offers the children an opportunity to apply the theme of the lesson in their daily lives. The answers suggested in the teacher's manual are not necessarily the answers the children will give, but we hope that you will be able to lead the discussion toward these or similar answers.

On the fifth day, you can choose from one of the art and craft projects suggested in the *Extending the Lesson* section. The materials needed for each project are listed separately. For some of these art projects, patterns are provided in the supplementary packet included with this teacher's manual. Each project is directly related either to the focus of the lesson or to one of the suggested stories. By working with their hands on these projects, the children are better able to retain the lesson concept. Included in this section is an action rhyme. This rhyme can be used during any of the class periods as a change of pace and to help channel the children's energies. Each class period should begin and conclude with prayer. The use of the formal prayers of the Church—the "Our Father", the "Hail Mary", and the "Glory Be"—is strongly encouraged. We have included short prayers written in the words of children. We hope that this format will encourage your students to offer their own spontaneous prayers along with the use of formal prayer.

Every attempt has been made to provide enough material in the lessons to fill four or five twenty- to thirty-minute class periods. In each lesson the children are stimulated in a variety of ways to increase their retention of the lesson.

The following is a suggested time schedule for this program in the kindergarten setting. Obviously, when working with kindergarten children, the time cannot be rigidly structured. You will want to adjust this model to fit your specific needs.

Day 1. Vocabulary Word(s) and Concepts of Faith
Day 2. Application and Discussion Questions
Day 3. Suggested Story and Review Questions
Day 4. Living the Lesson
Day 5. Art and Craft Project

Expansion material includes worksheets and additional stories, art and craft projects, and action rhymes.

Lesson Plans

Lesson 1   **There Is One God—Trinity**

Workbook Pages

Pre-school A. 1–2
Pre-school B. 53–54
Kindergarten 1–3

Lesson Focus

As Catholics, we believe there are three Persons in one God: Father, Son, and Holy Spirit. We show our belief in the Blessed Trinity every time we make the "Sign of the Cross". Even as adults, we cannot fully comprehend this basic concept of our Faith. We believe it is true because Jesus, Who is God the Son, revealed the Blessed Trinity to us in His teachings. Not even in heaven will the mystery of the Blessed Trinity be fully understood.

In presenting this lesson to the children, it should be emphasized that all three Persons in God are equal. Each Person is all-loving, all-powerful, all-wise, and so forth. There was never a time when all three Persons did not exist.

The vocabulary words are **Trinity**—we call the three Persons in one God "the Blessed Trinity" (which means "the holy Three")—and **mystery**—something we cannot fully understand. Even though we cannot completely understand the Blessed Trinity, we believe that there are three Persons in one God: Father, Son, and Holy Spirit. We believe this because Jesus taught us about the Blessed Trinity.

Concepts of Faith

How many Gods are there?
There is one God, and there are three Persons in the one God: Father, Son, and Holy Spirit.

What do we call the three Persons in one God?
We call the three Persons in one God "the Blessed Trinity".

Lesson Presentation

Application

Using the example of yourself or another adult, explain to the children the different roles you fulfill and the names to which you answer. For example, a man can be a son, a brother, a husband, a father, a teacher, and a Boy Scout leader. Some people call this man Mr. Jones or Tom Jones. His friends call him Tom, and his children call him Daddy. How many men are there? Of course, there is only one. There is only one man, but this one man can do and be many things to different people. A woman can be a daughter, a sister, a wife, a mother, a doctor, and a Girl Scout leader. She can be called Mrs. Jones, Mary Jones, Dr. Jones, Mary, or Mom. There is only one woman. Explain to the children that many names for the same person help us try to understand the Blessed Trinity. (You may wish to point out to the children that God the Father, God the Son, and God the Holy Spirit are not just other names we call God but three Persons in one God.) The Blessed Trinity is a mystery—something we cannot understand. We believe this mystery because Jesus told us about the Blessed Trinity.

The unity of persons in the family can be used as another imperfect example of the perfect unity of Persons in the Blessed Trinity. Ask the children how many families live in their house. Then ask the children how many people live in their house. Point out that one family has many people in it. Those people are all separate people, but there is still only one family. There are three Persons in one God. (Again, this does not come close to explaining the Blessed Trinity, but it does offer us a small comparison to use in teaching.)

Tell the children the names of the three Persons in the Blessed Trinity: God the Father, God the Son, and God the Holy Spirit. We usually think of God the Father as our Creator. He gave each of us life. The second Person of the Blessed Trinity is God the Son. He became man to show us and teach us how to live. Jesus is God the Son. He died for us. The third Person of the Blessed Trinity is God the Holy Spirit. He helps us act as images of God. The dove is a sign of the Holy Spirit. God the Father is God, God the Son is God, and God the Holy Spirit is God. There are three Persons in one God. We call these three Persons the Blessed Trinity.

Discussion Questions

1. **A man or a woman can be and do many different things for different people. How many persons in one man or one woman?** (One person.)
2. **How many Persons are there in God?** (There are three Persons in God—Father, Son, and Holy Spirit.)
3. **What do we call the three Persons in one God?** (The Blessed Trinity.)
4. **Will we ever completely understand the mystery of the Blessed Trinity?** (No, not even when we go to heaven.)
5. **Why do we believe there are three Persons in one God?** (Because Jesus, God the Son, taught us about the Blessed Trinity.)

Living the Lesson

Each time we make the "Sign of the Cross" we give praise to the three Persons of the Blessed Trinity. When we say the "Glory Be", we are showing that we believe that God always was and always will be.

Make the "Sign of the Cross" for the children, showing them that you touch your forehead saying "In the name of the Father", then your chest saying "and of the Son", then your left and right shoulders saying "and of the Holy Spirit". Then, turning your back to the children (so as not to confuse them as to which shoulder is first), have the children make the "Sign of the Cross" with you. Tell them that we make the "Sign of the Cross" before and after we pray. When we do this, we are telling God we believe in Him, and we are offering our prayers to Him.

Next, teach the children the "Glory Be". Explain that "glory" means praise and honor. We praise God for all His goodness. When we pray the "Glory Be", we show our love for God by praising the Blessed Trinity. Tell the children the "Glory Be" is a special prayer of praise we offer the Blessed Trinity. Have the children repeat each phrase after you. Then have them say it with you. "Glory be to the Father/ and to the Son/ and to the Holy Spirit/ as it was in the beginning/ is now and ever shall be/ world without end. Amen." It is suggested that the "Glory Be" be said in the children's daily prayers at school.

Review Questions

1. **When do we make the "Sign of the Cross"?** (Before and after we pray.)
2. **Why do we make the "Sign of the Cross"?** (To show God we believe in Him as the Blessed Trinity.)
3. **What is the special prayer to the Blessed Trinity?** (The "Glory Be".)

Extending the Lesson

Art and Craft Projects

Materials Needed
  A. Construction paper, mobile pattern provided, scissors, hole punch, yarn.
  B. Beads, chenille pipe cleaners, cross pattern provided.

  A. Trinity Mobile. Using the pattern provided, cut one of each object from construction paper for each child. Label each item as follows:

  Cloverleaf—There is one God.
  Sun—God the Father made the whole world.
  Cross—Jesus is God the Son.
  Dove—A sign of God the Holy Spirit.

Using the hole punch, make a hole at the top of all the objects. Also make a hole in the two bottom parts and in the stem of the cloverleaf. Cut four pieces of yarn (about 6 inches each) for each child. Thread one piece of yarn through the hole in each object. Then tie each object to the cloverleaf, threading the pieces of yarn through one of the holes in the bottom parts and in the stem. Thread the extra piece of yarn through the hole at the top of the cloverleaf to make a hanger. Remind the children that Father, Son, and Holy Spirit are not just other names we call God but are the three Persons in the Blessed Trinity. This is a mystery, and we cannot understand it. We believe it because Jesus, God the Son, taught us about the Blessed Trinity.
  B. Beaded Cross. Follow the directions on the pattern provided. Remind the children that we make the "Sign of the Cross" before and after we pray. We should make the "Sign of the Cross"

Use these patterns from the special pattern packet.

A.

B.

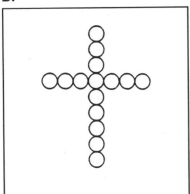

carefully, because it is a little prayer. We are telling God we believe in Him as the Blessed Trinity.

Action Rhyme

Look at my fingers. (*Hold up both hands.*)
Count them with me. (*One hand counts fingers on other hand.*)
How many fingers do you see? (*Wiggle fingers of both hands.*)
One, two, and three. (*Hold up one, then two, then three fingers.*)
Three Persons in God. (*Hold up three fingers.*)
One, two, and three. (*Count three fingers.*)
Three Persons of the Trinity. (*Make a triangle with thumbs and index fingers.*)
One, two, and three. (*Count three fingers.*)
Only one God. (*Hold up one finger.*)
He loves me. (*Hug self.*)
Three Persons in God. (*Hold up three fingers.*)
The Blessed Trinity.

Prayer

Have the children make the "Sign of the Cross" and pray the "Glory Be".

Worksheets

The worksheets can be sent home to be completed or can be completed in the classroom and then sent home. In either case, the worksheets should be used as take-home material because they furnish the basis for parent–child discussion.

Pre-school A. Worksheet 1 relates to the lesson theme and can be distributed to the children after the Application portion of the Lesson Presentation section to reinforce the concept. Worksheet 2 can be distributed after the Living the Lesson section to help the children relate the theme to their daily lives.

Pre-school B. Worksheet 53 can be distributed after the Living the Lesson section to help the children relate the theme to their daily lives. Worksheet 54 relates to the lesson theme and can be distributed to the children after the Application portion of the Lesson Presentation section to reinforce the concept.

Kindergarten. Worksheets 1 and 2 can be distributed after the Living the Lesson section to help the children relate the theme to their daily lives. Worksheet 3 relates to the lesson theme and may be distributed to the children after the Application portion of the Lesson Presentation section to reinforce the concept.

We See God in the World around Us—Creation

Workbook Pages
Pre-school A. 3–5
Pre-school B. 55–57
Kindergarten 4–6

Lesson Focus

To grow in the love of God, we first must come to know God and His love for us. Through creation, God reveals Himself to us as our loving and caring Father. In learning about God, we also come to know ourselves, because we are made in the image of God.

The vocabulary word **Creator** can be explained as a name for God, Who can make something out of nothing. Explain to the children that God made all the things that are alive and all the things that are not alive from nothing. As you present this lesson, the children should become aware of the wonders of God seen in all creation.

Concepts of Faith

Who made the world and everything in it?
God made the world and everything in it.

Who is our Creator?
God is our Creator.

Lesson Presentation

Application

Show the children an apple (or any fruit with seeds). Ask the children what they would have to do to made an apple grow. Cut the apple open to show the children the seeds. Explain to the children that, to make an apple grow, they would have to plant the seeds, water the tree, pull the weeds, and then, if they were lucky, an apple might grow on the tree. Apple trees grow from apple seeds. This is God's plan. God made the first fruit trees from nothing. We cannot make a tree without seeds.

Next, show the children a scenic picture of mountains, rivers, trees, sky, and so forth. Ask the children if they can make any of the things they see in the picture. Some of the children might say they could make a lake by putting lots of water in one place or a mountain by piling up lots of dirt. Point out to the children that they would have to use water and dirt that are already in the world. We could not make these things from nothing. God made the mountains and lakes from nothing. He made the whole world and everything in it for all the people. God made all the people to be in charge of the things in the world. More wondrous than all this, God loves each of us and has given us life through our parents. Because we are persons, we can love God, praise Him, and thank Him for all He has made.

Discussion Questions

1. **Who is the Creator of the world?** (God.)
2. **Can we make something from nothing?** (No, only God can.)
3. **Did God need seeds to make trees?** (No.) **Do we?** (Yes.)
4. **Was everything created by God?** (Yes.)

Suggested Story

"Creation" (based on Genesis 1:1–31)

Living the Lesson

We call God "Creator" because He made the world and everything in it from nothing. God made all the things in the world for people to use. We can use all the things God has made, but we cannot use other people. We love, praise, and thank God for the wonderful world He has given us.

1. **How can we show God we are thankful for our world?** (By taking care of our world—keeping the land, air, and water clean, by not littering, and so forth.)
2. **How do we use the things God made for us?** (Examples: water—to drink, to cook with, to wash in, to grow food, to play in, to make energy; the plants and trees—to eat, to give shade, to make houses and other things out of wood, to feed the animals; animals—to do work for us, to give us food, to have fun with; the sun—to give us energy, light, and warmth.)
3. Have the children make their own "thank you" prayer to God for the beautiful world He has given us. They can either draw pictures of what they are thankful for, or you may wish to write their thank you prayer on the board and then read it to them.

Extending the Lesson

Art and Craft Projects

Materials Needed

    A. Creation workbook pages, scissors, yarn, crayons, construction paper, hole punch.

    B. Construction paper, magazine pictures, brads, scissors, glue.

    C. Construction paper, glue, scissors, magazine pictures.

    A. Creation Booklet. A creation booklet can be made from the children's workbook pages. Have the children color the pictures. Cut a piece of construction paper into fourths and glue a picture to each piece. Then have the children place the pictures to show the order in which God created them. Punch holes on the left side of the pages. Lace with yarn and tie to make a booklet. The children can design their own covers. While they are working, remind them that God made the whole world and everything in it from nothing. God is our Creator and our loving Father.

B. Picture Wheel. For each child, cut two circles—each nine inches in diameter—from construction paper. Draw lines on both circles, dividing them into quarters. Cut out one quarter from one of the circles and set this circle aside to be the top of the picture wheel. Distribute magazines to the children and have them find and cut out four pictures of different things God created, for example, animals, plants, sun, moon, water, people. Glue these pictures in the four sections of the remaining circle, one picture in each section. This circle is the bottom of the picture wheel. Placing the top circle on the bottom circle, secure them in the center with a brad. As the children turn the top circle, a picture will appear in the cut-out section. The picture wheel can be labeled "God made the whole world and everything in it." As the children are working, remind them that God made the things in the world for people to use. We may use the things but not other people.

C. Hands and World Picture. For each child, cut one large circle from construction paper. This circle will be the world. Glue it to another, larger piece of paper. Have the children trace each other's hands, one hand on each side of the circle. Then have the children cut pictures from magazines or draw pictures of things God has made. Place these pictures on the "world". Label the picture "God made all things." Remind the children, while they are working, that only God can make something from nothing. He is our Creator and a loving Father.

Action Rhyme

Who made the fish? (*Hands together, moving back and forth in swimming motion.*)
Who made the seas? (*Hand moves up and down to show waves.*)
Who made the stars? (*Point up to sky.*)
Can you tell me? (*Point to others.*)
Who made the animals,
    big and small? (*Hand overhead, then down low.*)
Who made the people, (*Arms spread wide.*)
And loves them all? (*Hug self.*)
God made the fish, (*Swimming motion with hands.*)
The stars, and the seas. (*Wave motion with hands.*)
God made everything. (*Arms spread wide.*)
God made me. (*Point to self.*)

Prayer

Our Father in heaven, we thank You for the wonderful world You have given us. We love You. Amen.

Worksheets

The worksheets can be sent home to be completed or can be completed in the classroom and then sent home. In either case, the worksheets should be used as take-home material because they furnish the basis for parent–child faith discussion.

Pre-school A. Worksheets 3 and 4 can be used as suggested in the Art and Craft Projects of this lesson or they can be used after the Suggested Story to aid the children's retention of the story. Worksheet 5 can be distributed after the Application portion of the Lesson Presentation section to reinforce the concept, or they can be used after the Suggested Story.

Pre-school B. Worksheet 55 can be distributed to the children after the Application portion of the Lesson Presentation section to reinforce the concept, or they can be used after the Suggested Story. Worksheets 56 and 57 can be used as suggested in the Art and Craft Projects of this lesson, or they may be used after the Suggested Story to aid the children's retention of the story.

Kindergarten. Worksheets 4 and 5 can be used after the Suggested Story to aid the children's retention of the story. Worksheet 6 relates to the lesson theme and can be distributed to the children after the Application portion of the Lesson Presentation section to reinforce the concept.

Creation

In the beginning there was only God. God made everything from His love. He made the whole world and everything in it.

God made the angels to share heaven with Him. The angels are persons, like us, with a mind to think and a will to make choices. The angels do not have bodies, so we cannot see them.

Before God made the world, there was only darkness. Then God said, "Let there be light." He called the light day and the darkness night.

God made the blue sky. He made all the waters of the lakes, rivers, and oceans. He made the water be in some places and dry land in other places.

God covered the land with soft green grass, trees with fruit, and many kinds of flowers.

God made the sun to shine during the day and the moon and the stars to shine at night.

He filled the waters with fish and all kinds of swimming creatures. God filled the sky with birds, butterflies, and everything that flies.

God made every kind of animal, tame and wild, big and small. God made them all.

God looked at everything He had made and was pleased. Then God made the first man, Adam, and the first woman, Eve. God said, "I have made the whole world and everything in it for you. I give you all kinds of plants for food and all kinds of animals. You are in charge of all the things in the world." God looked at all He made and saw it was good and He was pleased.

God is with us always. He has given us life, the whole world, and everything in the world because He loves us. Every person, plant and animal, star and lake that we see should remind us of God, our Creator. We should love God and thank Him for everything He has made.

Review Questions

1. **Who made the world and everything in it?** (God.)
2. **Whom did God make first?** (The angels.)
3. **What did God make next?** (Day and night.)
4. **What did God make to shine during the day?** (The sun.)
5. **To whom did God give everything?** (Adam and Eve, the first man and woman.)

I Am Special to God Who Made Me

Workbook Pages
Pre-school A. 6–7
Pre-school B. 58–59
Kindergarten 7–9

Lesson Focus

We are all made in the image of God. This concept may cause some confusion in the children's minds. They may think that, since we are all made in the image of God, we look like God. This confusion can be clarified by pointing out physical differences among the children—for example, some have brown hair, some have blond, some blue eyes, some brown, some are tall, some are short—yet we are all made in the image of God. Even twins who strongly resemble each other have personal differences—one is quiet, one is talkative; one likes to eat something that the other does not like. We all reflect God in different ways. Stress that no one or two of us or even a million of us reflect God completely or accurately. We should want to reflect God as clearly as we are able.

The vocabulary word is **image**—the reflection of ourselves and others.

Concepts of Faith

Why are we special to God?
We are special because we are made in the image of God.

Lesson Presentation

Application

Begin by holding a large mirror toward the children. What they see is their reflection. Refer to this reflection as an image. Turning your back to the class, place the mirror in such a way that the children can see you in it. Change your expression (smile or frown), then ask the children to guess what you are doing. When they guess correctly, ask them how they know. They should respond that they can see you in the mirror. Your image in the mirror shows the children something about you. As images of God, we want to teach others about God and His love for us. The good things we "think, and say, and do" help others see and learn about God through us.

Discussion Questions

1. **Who made each of us?** (God.)
2. **How are we made?** (We are made in the image of God.)
3. **Are we all exactly alike?** (No.)
4. **Do we all reflect God in the same way?** (No, we all do things in a different way, but all the good things we "think, and say, and do" reflect God.)
5. **Have the children share some ways they act as an image of God.** (Pick up their toys, help their parents, share their toys.)

6. **Is everyone an image of God?** (Yes, but when we make the wrong choice and do things that we know are not right, we are not as clear an image of God—like the sun on a cloudy day.)

Suggested Stories

A. "Jesus and the Children" (based on Luke 18:15–17)
B. "Adam and Eve" (based on Genesis 1:26; 2:18–23)

Living the Lesson

We are all special because we are images of God. We can love and act the way God loves and acts. We can share God's life. When we make the wrong choices, we are not acting as images of God, but when we choose to act like God, we are like "mirrors". Other people can see God in us. We are clear and bright images of God.

1. **Why are we special?** (Because we are made in God's image.)
2. **Are the trees or animals images of God?** (No, they cannot think or choose.)
3. **List examples for the children of different situations. In which situations would they be reflecting God?** (Obeying parents, saying prayers, following school rules, fighting with a brother or a sister, not sharing toys, sitting quietly at church, and so forth.)
4. Ask the children to share some examples of how they show that they are made in the image of God at school, at home, at church, or at play.

Extending the Lesson

Art and Craft Projects

Materials Needed
    A. Mirror pattern, scissors, shiny foil, glue, construction paper, pencil.
    B. Paper doll pattern, shiny foil, lightweight cardboard, glue, pencil, crayons.
    C. Large paper, pencil, crayons, red construction paper, heart pattern, shiny foil, glue.

    A. Mirror. Using the pattern, cut one "mirror" for each child from construction paper. Have the children glue a circle of shiny foil to the center. Print around the edge of the mirror "I am a reflection of God." Remind the children that the mirror helps them remember that they reflect God to others.
    B. Paper Doll. Using the pattern, cut one paper doll for each child. Glue a circle of shiny foil over the face. Print "I am an image of God" across the chest of the paper doll. The paper doll can be colored by the children. The paper doll helps the children remember that only people are images of God.
    C. Life-sized Picture. Have the children lie on large pieces of

Use these patterns from the special pattern packet.

A.

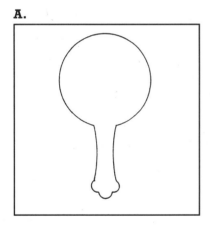

B.

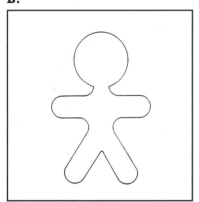

paper while you trace their bodies. Have them color the tracings to look like themselves. Remind them that they are special because God made them in His image. Glue a paper heart to the chest and remind the children they should love the way God loves. Glue a circular piece of foil to the face. Print "I am an image of God" around the foil. Remind the children that everything they "think, and say, and do" should reflect God.

Action Rhyme

I am special (*Point to self.*)
Because God made me. (*Point to heaven, then to self.*)
I'm not like the bunny (*Form ears on top of head with hands, and hop up and down.*)
Or the apple tree. (*Arms circle head and sway.*)
I can love and think, (*Hands on heart, then point to head.*)
I can talk and say (*Point to mouth.*)
"I love everybody." (*Arms spread wide.*)
God made me that way.

Prayer

Dear God, thank You for making me. Help me to be a reflection of You to everyone I meet.

Worksheets

The worksheets can be sent home to be completed or can be completed in the classroom and then sent home. In either case, the worksheets should be used as take-home material because they furnish the basis for parent–child faith discussion.

Pre-school A. Worksheet 6 relates to the lesson theme and can be distributed to the children after the Application portion of the Lesson Presentation section to reinforce the concept. Worksheet 7 may be used after the Suggested Story to aid the children's retention of the story.

Pre-school B. Worksheet 58 can be used after the Suggested Story to aid the children's retention of the story. Worksheet 59 can be distributed after the Living the Lesson section to help the children relate the theme to their daily lives.

Kindergarten. Worksheets 7 and 9 can each be used after its related Suggested Story to aid the children's retention of the story. Worksheet 8 relates to the lesson theme and can be distributed to the children after the Application portion of the Lesson Presentation section to reinforce the concept.

Jesus and the Children

When Jesus was living on earth, there were no cars, or buses, or even bicycles. Jesus traveled from one town to another on foot. He walked many miles with His friends. He wanted all the people to hear about God and to know about His love.

One day, Jesus was sitting on a hillside teaching many people about God. Some mothers heard that Jesus was near their neighborhood.

"We want to take you to see Jesus", the mothers told their children. "Jesus is a great teacher. He can teach you about God."

So off they went to walk to the hill where Jesus was teaching. When they got there, they could hardly believe their eyes! There were people everywhere! People were sitting under trees, and people were sitting on the hill. There were even people standing in the road. Slowly and patiently, the mothers helped the children through the crowd. The children could not see Jesus, because all the grownups were so tall. Finally, the mothers and their children made their way to the front of the crowd. They could see Jesus now! He was sitting with His special helpers. As the mothers and the children came close to Jesus, the helpers stopped them.

"Can't you see Jesus is busy?" they said. "Jesus does not have time for your children now."

Sadly, the mothers began to leave with their children. But Jesus saw what had happened.

"Let the children come to me", Jesus said. "Do not send them away."

Quickly the children ran to Jesus. He laid His hands on their heads, blessing them. Then He lifted the littlest child onto His lap.

"All of you must come to God with hearts full of love like these children. They love the way God does."

The children had a wonderful time with Jesus. They listened to all He had to say. The mothers and the children went home happy that they had seen Jesus and learned more about God's great love.

We are all God's children. He made us in His image. He wants us to reflect Him by loving and caring for each other. By doing this, we show in a small way God's great love for us.

Review Questions

1. **Who came to see Jesus?** (The mothers and the children.)
2. **What did Jesus' helpers say to the mothers?** (Go away, Jesus is busy.)
3. **Why did Jesus want the children to stay?** (Because they had hearts full of love, and they reflected God's love.)

4. **Who are God's children?** (All of us.)
5. **Are we all images of God?** (Yes, even if we make the wrong choices and do not act as an image of God. Then we are not as bright an image of God, but we are still an image of God.)
6. **Whom do we act like when we show our love for other people?** (God.)

Adam and Eve

After God made the angels, He made the world and all the plants and animals. God then made Adam, the first man. Adam was special because he was made in the image of God. Adam did not look like God, but he could love and work like God. He could also share God's life.

God had some work for Adam to do. All the animals that God made needed names. God asked Adam to name them. Adam obeyed God because he loved God very much. Adam looked at all the animals as he was naming them and saw that he was different from them. Adam knew he was special. He could think and make choices, but the animals could not. He could act like God, but the animals could not. Only Adam was made in the image of God. Only Adam was a person.

Adam loved God and took care of God's world, but Adam was very lonely. There was no one to share God's love with Adam. He was the only person God made with a body. The angels were persons, but they did not have bodies. The animals had bodies, but they were not persons. Poor Adam was very lonesome!

God knew it was not good for Adam to be alone, so He made the first woman. Her name was Eve. Eve did not look exactly like Adam, but she was made in the image of God, just like Adam. She was a person too. Adam and Eve could love each other with a God-like love. Best of all, they could grow as a family in God's love.

Review Questions

1. **Who was the first man?** (Adam.)
2. **What did God ask Adam to do?** (Name the animals.)
3. **Who was the first woman?** (Eve.)
4. **Why did God make Eve?** (To love God and to love Adam as God did.)
5. **Why did God make Adam?** (To love God and to love Eve as God did.)
6. **Did Adam and Eve look like God?** (No.)
7. **How were Adam and Eve different from the animals?** (They could think and make choices—they were persons.)
8. **How were Adam and Eve like God?** (They were both made in the image of God to do what God does—love and work.)

Lesson 4   Actions and Attitudes—
The Ten Commandments

Workbook Pages

Pre-school A. 8–9
Pre-school B. 60–61
Kindergarten 10–12

Lesson Focus

Remind the children of the last lesson—we are all made in the image of God. Mention that the "image" in the mirror has no choice. It has to do whatever the person in front of the mirror does. God has given us a free will. We do not have to act as an image of God. We can choose to act or not to act as an image of God. How do we know how God acts? God gave us the Ten Commandments to help us know how to live as an image of God. They are a way of life for an image of God. When we choose to act as an image of God by following the commandments, we show our love for God. The commandments are not rules or laws forced on us but rather the way an image of God chooses to act. Our actions—the things we do—and our attitudes—how we think—both should show that we love God. We were made to know, love, and serve God in all we "think, and say, and do".

Commandments is the vocabulary word. The commandments should be explained as God's way of helping us know how to act as an image of God. They help us make the right choices. They are the way an image of God should live.

Concepts of Faith

How should we show our love for God?

We should show our love for God by choosing to follow the commandments that He gave us.

Lesson Presentation

Application

Begin by having the children pretend that you are holding two ice cream cones (or hold up pictures of two ice cream cones). The cones should be two different flavors, for example, one chocolate and one strawberry. Ask the children what would happen if both cones were offered to a dog. The dog would probably eat both, not caring about the flavors.

But what would happen if the two cones were offered to one of the children? Give a few of the children a chance to choose one of the cones. Explain: God made us in His image. We have minds to think and wills to choose. We can choose between right and wrong. We can choose to act or not to act as images of God. We are always images of God, even when we make the wrong choice. But we are not as bright an image of God—like the sun on a cloudy day—when we choose to do wrong.

How do we know if the choice we make is a right choice or a wrong choice? God gave us the Ten Commandments to help us make good choices and to teach us how an image of God lives. Introduce the Ten Commandments now. The following children's version might be easier for them to understand:

"Thee is only one God and you should love Him with all your heart. Keep God's name holy. Go to church on Sunday. Obey your mom and dad. Be kind to other people. You should love everyone as an image of God. Do not take things that do not belong to you. You should tell the truth. Do not be jealous of other people. Do not be jealous of the things other people have."

The Ten Commandments may also be explained to the children as a set of directions. If the children were invited to a friend's home, they would need to know where their friend lived—what direction to go, what street their friend lived on. In general, they would need to know how to find their friend's house. God invites us to come to Him in heaven. The Ten Commandments show us the way so we do not get lost. We can choose to act as an image of God by making the right choices and following the Ten Commandments.

Discussion Questions

1. **Who is made in the image of God?** (Everyone.)
2. **How do we know how an image of God should act?** (The Ten Commandments.)
3. **What do the Ten Commandments help us do?** (Live as an image of God, making the right choices.)
4. **When we make wrong choices, are we still an image of God?** (Yes, but we are not acting as we should. We are not as clear or bright an image of God.)

Suggested Stories

A. "The Rich Young Man" (based on Matthew 19:16–22)
B. "Moses and the Ten Commandments" (based on Exodus 20:1–17)

Living the Lesson

It is not always easy to do what is right and to make right choices. If we ask ourselves what an image of God would do, it is easier to know what is right. We should try very hard to live by the Ten Commandments.

1. **Where are some places we have to make choices about how to act?** (At home, at school, and at church.)
2. Have the children give examples from their own lives of how they can live each of the Ten Commandments. Use the children's version of the commandments.

First Commandment
   There is only one God, and you should love Him with all your heart. (We should say our prayers.)

Second Commandment

Keep God's name holy. (We should not say bad words.)

Third Commandment

Go to church on Sunday. (We should not misbehave in church.)

Fourth Commandment

Obey your mom and dad. (We should obey our parents and teachers.)

Fifth Commandment

Be kind to other people. (We should not hurt other people.)

Sixth Commandment

You should love everyone as an image of God. (We should love other persons in the right way.)

Seventh Commandment

Do not take things that do not belong to you. (We do not take things from stores or from our friends.)

Eighth Commandment

You should tell the truth. (We should not tell lies.)

Ninth Commandment

Do not be jealous of other people. (We should not be jealous of how other people look or what they can do.)

Tenth Commandment

Do not be jealous of the things other people have. (We should not be jealous of the toys or nice things that other people have.)

3. **Which of the Ten Commandments help us to love and serve God better?** (1, 2, and 3.)

4. **Which help us know how to love and serve each other better?** (4, 5, 6, 7, 8, 9, and 10.)

Extending the Lesson

Art and Craft Projects

Materials Needed

A. For each child, a sheet of paper with the Ten Commandments typed on it, tongue depressors, construction paper, glue, scissors.

B. Lightweight cardboard, foil, scissors, list of Ten Commandments for each child.

C. List of Ten Commandments for each child, glue, scissors.

A. Ladder to Heaven. Give each child a sheet of paper with the children's Ten Commandments typed or written on it. Have the children cut the commandments out in strips. Glue tongue depressors or construction paper strips in the form of a ladder with ten rungs. Glue one commandment on each rung. If the commandments are numbered, the children can keep the commandments in the right order by recognizing the correct number. The entire project can be glued to a full piece of construction paper with the phrase "Ladder to heaven" written on each finished project.

B. Stone Tablets. Cut out of lightweight cardboard a set of "stone tablets" for each child. Have the children cover the tablets with foil. Give each child a sheet of paper with the children's Ten Commandments typed or written on it. Have the children cut the commandments out in strips. If the commandments are numbered, the children can keep the commandments in the right order by recognizing the correct number. Have the children glue the commandment strips on the foil-covered tablets. The finished project can be labeled "How to act as an image of God".

C. Ten Commandments Chain. Type or write the children's Ten Commandments on a sheet of paper. Under each commandment write something the children can do that fits that commandment. For example, the first Commandment could read: "There is only one God and you should love Him with all your heart. Today in your prayers tell God you love Him." The Second Commandment could read: "Keep God's name holy. Today tell God thank you for making the world and all the beautiful things in it." Third Commandment: "Go to church on Sunday. Today say an extra prayer." Fourth Commandment: "Obey your mom and dad. Today pick up your toys without being asked." Fifth Commandment: "Be kind to other people. Today share your toys with a friend." Sixth Commandment: "You should love everyone as an image of God. Today tell your family that you love them." Seventh Commandment: "Do not take things that do not belong to you. Today draw a happy picture to give as a gift to someone." Eighth Commandment: "You should tell the truth. Today say only nice things about other people." Ninth Commandment: "Do not be jealous of other people. Today say something kind to a friend." Tenth Commandment: "Do not be jealous of the things other people have. Today say thank you to God for all you have." Have the children cut out each strip (containing the commandment and the activity) and glue the strips, in order, to strips of construction paper. Form a chain with the construction paper strips and have the children tear off a strip every day and do what it says.

Action Rhyme

> God gave the Ten Commandments to me (*Hold up ten fingers.*)
> So an image of God you will see. (*Hand circles face.*)
> I should want to think and love and say (*Point to head, heart, then mouth.*)
> Everything right in the best way. (*Shake finger.*)
> And if I choose to disobey and not do what is right, (*Point finger to self, then shake finger.*)
> The image of God that I am won't be bright. (*Cover the face with hands.*)
> So it's important, don't you see (*Shake finger and point to eyes.*)
> To follow God's commandments so we can be (*Make walking motion with fingers.*)
> Bright images of God for all to see. (*Open arms wide.*)

Prayer

Dear God, I love You. Help me to follow Your commandments and make the right choices. I want to be a bright image of God. I want to be with You in heaven. Amen.

Worksheets

The worksheets can be sent home to be completed or can be completed in the classroom and then sent home. In either case, the worksheets should be used as take-home material because they furnish the basis for parent–child faith discussion.

Pre-school A. Worksheet 8 can be distributed after the Living the Lesson section to help the children relate the theme to their daily lives. Worksheet 9 relates to the lesson theme and can be distributed to the children after the Application portion of the Lesson Presentation section to reinforce the concept.

Pre-school B. Worksheet 60 relates to the lesson theme and can be distributed to the children after the Application portion of the Lesson Presentation section to reinforce the concept. Worksheet 61 can be used after the Suggested Story to aid the children's retention of the story.

Kindergarten. Worksheet 10 can be distributed after the Living the Lesson section to help the children relate the theme to their daily lives. Worksheet 11 relates to the lesson theme and can be distributed to the children after the Application portion of the Lesson Presentation section to reinforce the concept. Worksheet 12 can be used after its related Suggested Story to aid the children's retention of the story.

The Rich Young Man

What is more important: money, food, things, or God?

There was once a very rich young man who came to talk to Jesus. This young man had lots of money. He bought all kinds of fancy clothes and lots and lots of good food. He bought many things with his money.

The young man wanted to follow Jesus and learn more about the things Jesus taught. The young man wanted to please God so he could go to heaven.

"Jesus", asked the young man, "what should I do so I can share in God's life now and in heaven?"

Jesus said, "You should obey the Ten Commandments." The young man wanted to do more. "What else can I do?" he asked. Jesus said, "Go sell everything you have and give your money to the poor people. Your treasure will be in heaven. Then come back and follow me."

The rich young man went away very sad. He liked having lots of money and lots of things. He did not want to give them away. He loved his money and all the things that he owned more than he loved God and more than heaven.

God wants us to show our love by following the Ten Commandments. He wants us to be the best image of God we can be. We should show our love for God in all we "think, and say, and do".

Review Questions

1. **Was the young man in the story rich or poor?** (He was rich—he had lots of money.)
2. **What did the young man ask Jesus?** (How he could get to heaven.)
3. **What was he first thing Jesus told the young man to do?** (He should follow the Ten Commandments.)
4. **What else did Jesus tell the young man to do?** (Sell his things and give away his money.)
5. **Did the young man do that?** (No.)
6. **Why not?** (Because things were more important to him than God.)
7. **Was the young man happy?** (No, he went away sad.)

Moses and the Ten Commandments

God chose a man named Moses to help the slaves in Egypt. The slaves were being punished by the King because they loved God.

"Moses, I want you to help the slaves", God said. "They are my chosen people. Tell them I have sent you."

At first Moses was afraid. "How can I help these people?" Moses asked. "I am only one man, and the King will never listen to me."

"Do not be afraid", God told him. "I will be with you always. I will give you the help you need."

Moses listened to God and obeyed Him. Moses told the King that God wanted the slaves to be free, but the King would not listen to Moses.

"The slaves should love and serve me", said the King, "but they only love and serve God. I will not set them free."

Again and again Moses asked the King to free the slaves, and, finally, the King agreed. Moses then led the chosen people of God across the desert to the place that God had ready for them. In that place there was a huge mountain called Sinai. It was a holy mountain. God asked Moses to climb to the top of the mountain. Moses obeyed God and climbed to the very top.

Moses and all the people were made in the image of God. They wanted to know how to act as images of God. God loved the people and wanted to help them live as His images. So God gave Moses the Ten Commandments to help all the people. Moses and the people knew if they followed the Ten Commandments they would be living as images of God.

Moses listened to God and wrote all His commandments on two stone tablets. Then Moses carried the stone tablets down the mountain. He showed the commandments of God to the people.

Moses told the people that the Ten Commandments would tell them how to love and serve God and how to share God's love with each other. Moses told the people, "The commandments will help us know how to live. They can help us get to heaven."

These same Ten Commandments help us today. They help us know what is right. When we choose to obey the Ten Commandments, we are acting as images of God.

Review Questions

1. **What did God ask Moses to do?** (Help the slaves.)
2. **Was this easy for Moses to do?** (No.)
3. **Did Moses make a good choice?** (Yes, he obeyed God.)
4. **What did God give to Moses?** (The Ten Commandments.)
5. **Why did God give the Ten Commandments to Moses?** (So everyone would know how to act as images of God.)

Lesson 5   Love Others As God Loves You

Workbook Pages

Pre-school A. 10–11
Pre-school B. 62–63
Kindergarten 13–15

Lesson Focus

God first loved us through creation, but even more wondrous was the great love shown through the very act of redemption. Jesus gave us the ultimate gift of love, His life. Through the Eucharist, He continually shares with us the special gift of His love, which enables us to grow in love for Him and others.

As God's images, we all have the need to love and be loved. Love is not an emotion (although it includes the emotions), but a total union of the wills of two or more persons. Persons love each other by making a gift of themselves to one another in their wills. Such a love is total, permanent, and life-giving. There are different kinds of love, for example, the love of a husband and wife, the love of children, and the solitary love of a hermit (united to the Church) praying for the world. It is impossible to love God without loving others, and it is impossible to love others without moving nearer to God.

The vocabulary word **love** can be explained as choosing to help everyone, including ourselves, be the best image of God we can be. Point out to the children that the word "love" is often used in the wrong way. Sometimes we say "I love my dog" (or cat, and so forth). But that is not quite true. We do not care about our pets in the same way that we love our moms and dads or other people. People are made in the image of God. They have minds and wills. They can act like God. Animals do not have minds and wills. They are not persons. They are not made in the image of God as persons are. We can truly love only other persons. We can care about our pets very much, but we do not truly love them. Sometimes we say "I love pizza" (or ice cream, and so forth). But this is not really quite true either. We can really enjoy a certain kind of food, but we do not really love it. We can love only persons.

Concepts of Faith

Whom does God love?
God loves everyone.

Whom are we to love?
We are to love God, ourselves, and everyone else.

Lesson Presentation

Application

For this lesson, you may want to have pictures of a bride and groom, a family, a priest, nuns in various habits, and a brother.

Explain to the children that God loves. God loves us; God loves everyone.

We are made in the image of God to do what God does. That means that, because God loves us and everyone, we should love ourselves and everyone else. First, we should love God, then we should love others as God loves us.

There are many ways to show this love for others. Some ways are big and difficult for us. Some are smaller and easier to do. As we grow up, we choose how we will lives our lives and show our love of God and of others. We are all called by God to love others in different ways. Some people answer God's call and show their love by getting married and becoming husbands and wives, moms and dads. (Show a picture of a bride and groom.) The people who choose to show their love by being married help themselves and their families lead good lives so they can be happy now and happy together in heaven someday. (Show a picture of a family.)

Some people choose not to get married. They answer God's call and show their love for others in different ways. Some men become priests. (Show a picture of a priest.) They share their love with all of us, helping themselves and all of us to lead good lives now and to get to heaven. Other men and women answer God's call and share their love in another way. Some of the women live, work, and pray together. They are called "sisters". (Show a picture of nuns in various habits.) The sisters teach in schools, work in hospitals, and take care of the poor. They show their love in many ways. Certain men also answer God's call and share their love in this way. They are called "brothers". (Show a picture of a brother.) The brothers live, work, and pray together, too. They show their love of God by teaching and by helping the poor and the sick. Some people choose not to marry or become priests, sisters, or brothers. They live their lives loving God and loving others too.

All these people are living their lives as images of God, loving others as God loves them. They are all sharing their love as images of God should. We all have a special way to live and share our love with others. When we love others, we make ourselves happy, because we are acting as God made us to act.

Discussion Questions

1. **What does God do?** (God loves.)
2. **Whom does God love?** (Everyone.)
3. **Because we are made in the image of God, what are we to do?** (Love as God loves.)
4. **Whom are we to love?** (God, ourselves, and everyone.)
5. **Can we love our pets?** (No, they are not persons made in the image of God. We care for our pets because God made them for us.)
6. **Can we love certain foods?** (No, not the way we love persons.)
7. **What are some ways people can answer God's call and live their love?** (By getting married, by not getting married, by becoming a priest, by becoming a sister, by becoming a brother.)

Suggested Stories

A. "The Poor Woman Who Showed Her Love" (based on Mark 12:41–44)

B. "The Stranger Who Turned into a Friend" (based on Luke 10:30–37)

Living the Lesson

It is important that the children understand that loving others does not mean loving only people in our family and our friends, but all God's family. One way to demonstrate this idea is to have the children participate in a food shelf program.

Ask the children if they ever get hungry. What do they do when they are hungry? (Ask their moms if they can have something to eat.) Explain to the children that there are people who do not have enough to eat. They cannot just go into their cupboards or refrigerators and get something to eat, because there is no food there. Ask the children how they could show their love for these people. (Say prayers, share food.) Have each child bring a non-perishable food item to share with the hungry people. (You may want to have extra items on hand, in case one of the children forgets.) The food collected can then be given to the local food shelf or community food share program.

We are never too little to share our love with others. We can show our love in little ways every day. List some of the ways we act as images of God, loving others as God loves us. (Letting others be first in line, saying "thank you", helping our moms and dads, forgiving others, not always getting our way but doing what others want, praying for sick people, being nice to someone who is lonely, helping someone who cannot do things as well as we can, sharing our toys or clothes or food with people who do not have any, and so forth.)

Extending the Lesson

Art and Craft Project

Materials Needed

A. Red construction paper, glue, scissors, sticker picture of God.

B. Dark construction paper, baby powder (finger paint is optional), glue, red paper heart for each child, container for powder or paint, hair spray.

C. Half-pint milk cartons, pipe cleaners, scissors, glue, stapler, scraps of different colored paper, 24 small paper hearts for each child.

A. "We Love Others as God Loves Us" Picture. Cut two hearts of the same size for each child. In the center of one of the hearts, draw a small rectangle. Cut the rectangle on three sides to form a "door". Fold the door so it stands open. Glue the two hearts together. Do not glue the door. Let it stand open. Place a sticker picture of God inside the door area. Write on the heart "We love others as God loves us." Remind the children that God loves each of us. To act as images of God, we are to do what God does. We are to love. We love God first, then ourselves, then we love others as God loves us.

B. "Handprints and Heart Picture". Give each child a dark-colored piece of construction paper and a red paper heart. Laying the construction paper lengthwise, have the children glue the heart in the center of the paper. The children will be placing handprints on either side of the heart. Handprints can be done in two ways: (1) Place a large amount of baby powder in a container, have the children place their hands, palms down, in the powder. Then have the children place their hands on the dark paper, pushing down to form a handprint. Spray the handprint lightly with hair spray to keep it from smearing. (2) Place finger paint in a container. Have the children place their hands, one at a time, into the paint. Then have the children place their hands on the dark paper, pushing down to form a handprint. Write on the heart "We are never too small to show our love for God." Remind the children that there are many little things we can do every day to show that we love others as God loves us.

C. Baskets of Love. Cut the tops off small (half-pint) milk cartons. The bottom portions of the cartons are to be used as a "basket". Use a pipe cleaner or strip of construction paper for a handle. Staple handle in place. Have the children tear small pieces of different colored paper to glue on the outside of the basket (or have them decorate the outside any way they wish). Provide the children with 24 small paper hearts, which are to be placed in the basket. Explain to the children that this is a basket of love to be shared with family and friends. They may give a heart to someone and then do something nice or say something kind to that person. In that way they are sharing their love. (You may wish to print on each heart "I love you" or "God loves you".) Remind the children that God loves everyone. To act as images of God, we are to love everyone, too.

Action Rhyme

I have something to share, (*Cup one hand over the other.*)
You have it, too. (*Point to others.*)
The more you share it, the bigger it grows. (*Move hands apart to show growing.*)
It's the gift of love. (*Hand on heart.*)
To love one another is easy to do. (*Nod head "yes".*)
Share your love with others, and they'll share their love with you. (*Arms out, as to give, then crossed over chest.*)

Prayer

Dear God, help us act as Your image, loving others as You love us. We offer You our acts of love. Amen.

Worksheets

The worksheets can be sent home to be completed or can be completed in the classroom and then sent home. In either case, the worksheets should be used as take-home material because they furnish the basis for parent–child faith discussion.

Pre-school A. Worksheet 10 may be used after the Suggested Story to aid the children's retention of the story. Worksheet 11 relates to the lesson theme and can be distributed to the children after the Application portion of the Lesson Presentation section to reinforce the concept or after the Living the Lesson section to help the children relate the theme to their daily lives.

Pre-school B. Worksheet 62 relates to the lesson theme and can be distributed to the children after the Application portion of the Lesson Presentation section to reinforce the concept. Worksheet 63 can be used after the Suggested Story to aid the children's retention of the story.

Kindergarten. Worksheets 13 and 14 can each be used after its related Suggested Story to aid the children's retention of the story. Worksheet 15 can be distributed after the Living the Lesson section to help the children relate the theme to their daily lives.

The Poor Woman Who Showed Her Love

Jesus was a teacher. He came to teach us how to live as images of God. One day, Jesus went to the temple with His friends. A temple is something like a church. Jesus and His friends were watching the people come into the temple. One by one, the people would put coins into a basket. This money was the people's gift to be shared by the poor.

Jesus watched a very rich man come into the temple. The rich man acted as if he were very important. He wore very fancy clothes. The rich man jingled his money very loudly. "I have lots of money", the man thought to himself. "But I will keep most of it for myself. I want to buy more clothes, and I want to go on a big trip. Oh, and I have to buy a fancier house. I'll just give to the poor what I have left over after I have my fun." When he thought everyone was looking at him, he put his coins in the basket. Even though there were a large number of coins, the gift was not as big a gift as he could have given.

Then a very poor woman came into the temple. She was dressed in old clothes. She reached into her pocket and took out two coins. They were the last two coins she had. Quietly, she put them into the basket. She bowed her head and prayed, "Please help the people who have even less than I do. Help me show my love to others as You have shown Your love to me."

When Jesus saw what had happened, He told His friends, "The poor woman gave more than the rich man did. The poor woman loved God so much that she gave all she had, while the rich man gave only his extra money."

God loves us with His whole Self. Everything we have comes from God, even our very lives. If we want to be the best images of God we can be, then we are to love as God loves. We should show our love for God in all we "think, and say, and do".

Review Questions

1. **What is a temple?** (Something like a church.)
2. **What did people do when they came into the temple?** (Put money into a basket.) **What was the money for?** (To help the poor people.)
3. **Who gave the most money?** (The rich man.)
4. **Whose gift showed more love?** (The poor woman's gift.) **Why?** (Because she gave all she had, and the rich man gave only his extra money.)
5. **When we show our love for others, whom are we reflecting?** (God.)

The Stranger Who Turned into a Friend

One day, Jesus told a story about a traveler who had been walking down a long and dusty road. The traveler was hurt and had lost all his food and money. The poor traveler could go no farther. He lay down by the side of the road. Soon a man came by carrying a bottle of water.

"Please help me", the traveler said. "I am thirsty and hurt."

But the man with the water did not stop. "I'm in a hurry", he said. "Besides, you have nothing to give me for my water."

The traveler felt very sad as he watched the man walk away. The traveler wondered if anyone coming along the road would help him. After a while, a merchant passed the traveler.

"Please help me", the traveler cried.

"But I do not even know you", the merchant said. "You should ask someone you know." And off he went.

The sun was going down, and soon it would be dark. The traveler still had found no one to help him. Just then a stranger from another place came by, riding on a donkey. He saw the traveler and felt sorry for him.

"Let me help you", the stranger said. The stranger gave the traveler water to drink, and he put bandages on the traveler's bruises. The stranger let the traveler ride on the donkey.

"You can stay with me at the inn", the stranger said. "I will buy you some food to eat and take care of you."

The traveler was very happy. "You are good and loving", he said to the stranger. "I will never forget you."

We should be like the stranger, showing our love by helping others. We should not ask for rewards for the good things we do or say. We should help others, even those we do not know. We should not say that we are too busy to help. When we show our love for others, we are showing we love God, and we also make ourselves happy.

Review Questions

1. **What happened to the traveler?** (He was hurt and had lost all his food and money.)
2. **What did the traveler need?** (Someone to help him.)
3. **What did the first man say to the traveler?** (He was too busy to help.)
4. **What did the merchant say to the traveler?** (He did not know the traveler.)
5. **What did the stranger from another place do?** (He helped the traveler. The stranger put bandages on his bruises, gave him water, put him on his donkey, took him to the inn, and bought him food.)
6. **Who was acting as an image of God?** (The stranger from another place.)
7. **When we help others, what do we show?** (We show we love others as God loves us.)

Lesson 6   God's House—The Church

Workbook Pages

Pre-school A. 12–13
Pre-school B. 64–65
Kindergarten 16–18

Lesson Focus

In this lesson, which is a presentation of a church, special care should be used not to confuse the children when using the term "church". In this lesson, the term "church" is used to refer to the physical building. The term "God's family" is used to refer to the members of the Church. In the lesson on Baptism, the idea of God's family will be presented in more detail. From this lesson the children should come to respect the items found in church and come to know the correct behavior for church.

The vocabulary word is **church** and should be explained to the children as "God's house on earth". (The words "on earth" are added to eliminate any confusion with heaven, where God lives with the angels, the saints, and all people who have lived good lives and have died.) To emphasize the respect given to the things found in a church, show the children a comic book and a Lectionary. After explaining that the Lectionary contains prayers and stories about God and is used in church, ask the children which is more important. Show the children a crucifix and a picture of animals (or any picture or poster), and then ask the children which is more important. The purpose of this activity is to help the children recognize that a certain respect is given to the things that pertain to God and to the things found in God's house.

This discussion leads directly to the behavior expected in church. God's house is a place of prayer and celebration. God's family gathers together to say "thank you" and to give praise to God. Mass is our most important prayer. Going to Mass is a special event in our lives. At Mass, stories about God are read, and God gives us the gift of Himself at Communion. Sitting quietly and listening to the stories about God, saying prayers, singing the songs, and showing respect for the things found in God's house can be gifts of love offered to God. There are many people at church, so we must be careful not to bother other people. When we are visiting a friend's house, we always try to do what is right. When we play with a friend's toys, we are very careful not to break them. This is similar to the way we should behave in God's house. We should be careful with the books and other things we see in church. We should remember that God is in church with us in a very special way.

Concepts of Faith

What is God's house on earth called?
God's house on earth is called the church.

Lesson Presentation

Application

To reinforce the discussion of a church, choose one or both of the following options.

Option 1

Take slides or pictures of your parish church to show the children. Include some of the following items:

1. **Altar:** The special table used at Mass.
2. **Candle on the altar:** It helps us remember that God is with us.
3. **Lectionary:** The special book used at Mass that has stories about God. (Tell the children that they should be sitting quietly and listening when people are reading from this big book.)
4. **Pew:** The benches we sit on in church. (Ask the children: Do you have rules about the furniture at home? Can you stand or walk on the chairs with your shoes on? This is God's house. You should not stand or walk on the pews, the benches. Remember that you should be praying or sitting quietly so the people around you can pray.)
5. **Pulpit:** The place where the priest stands and reads a story to us about God. (Tell the children that sometimes a woman or a man stands here and reads to us too. When someone is reading or talking, we should be quiet so everyone can hear. If we are talking, we cannot hear what is being said and neither can the people around us.)
6. **Chalice:** The special cup the priest uses at Mass.
7. **Chalice, paten, and host:** This is the special cup with a special plate that is used at Mass. (Tell the children that the white circle on the special plate is called a host.)
8. **Stained-glass window:** The windows in church with colored pictures on them.
9. **Organ:** This is like a big piano and makes the music we hear in church.
10. **Vestments:** The special clothes the priest wears when he says Mass. (Ask the children if they wear the same clothes to go to church or go to a party that they wear to play outside. Usually, you wear good or dress-up clothes to church and play clothes outside. When the priest goes to church, he wears special clothes too. They are called vestments and come in different colors—white, black, purple, green, and red. The priest wears different colors at different times during the year.)
11. **The parish priest(s):** Tell the children the priests' names and have the children repeat the names.
12. **The outside of the parish church:** Tell the children the name of the church. (Tell the children that this is a Catholic church. When we were babies and were baptized in the Catholic Church, we became Catholics. There are lots of Catholic churches everywhere in the world, and this parish is just one of them.)

Addition: You also may wish to include in the presentation a picture of the tabernacle and a picture of the collection basket or plate. Explain to the children that the Communion Hosts are kept in the tabernacle. God is with us in a very special way in the tabernacle. Explain to the children that the money put in the collection basket goes to help our church, all of us in the parish, and the poor people.

If your parish church has a prominent crucifix, show a picture of it to the children, explaining that the crucifix reminds us that Jesus died for us. If your church has a prominent statue, you could also show the children a picture of it, explaining its significance.

If you cannot take slides or photos of the items found in church, you may be able to find pictures of these items in various books to show to the children. During the explanation of the pictures, the respect given to the church and to the items found in it should be emphasized. Also, the kind of behavior expected at church should be stressed. (Some children may be confused about who the priests are. Because they see the priests in God's house, often the children think the priests are God or Jesus. It should be stated that the priests are men who are not married, but they offer their lives to God and do His work. They give themselves to God's family by saying Mass, by leading us in prayer, and by helping us learn more about God.)

Option 2
Take the children on a tour of the church, showing them the items listed under option 1. By actually seeing the items as they are in church, the children will be better able to retain the lesson material.

To both options, a picture of the current Pope and the bishop of your diocese should be added. The children should learn the name of the Pope and know that he serves as the leader of the Catholic Church today. Explain to the children that the Pope lives far away and cannot come to teach everyone about God because he is only one person, and there are so many people to teach. The bishop knows what the Pope wants taught, and he teaches the people in our area.

Discussion Questions

1. **Why do we go to church?** (To pray, to go to Mass, to hear stories about God, to be close to God in a special way.)
2. **How should we treat the things we see in God's house?** (We should be careful of the things we find in God's house.)
3. **How do we sit in church?** (Quietly, so we can pray, and so we do not disturb other people.)
4. **Should we walk on the pews or bring toys and snacks into church?** (No, we should listen, watch, pray, and sit quietly.)
5. **Do we go to church only on Sunday?** (No, we can go to church on any day. On Sunday and certain special days, called "holy days", we should go to church.)

Living the Lesson

We all belong to God's family. We join together in church to pray, to sing, and to praise God.

1. Show the children pictures of some of the things they saw in church. Ask the children if they can remember the name of the special cup the priest uses at Mass, the name of the benches at church, the name of the special clothes the priest wears at Mass, the name of the special table, and so forth.

2. **What is the name of our parish church? What is (are) the names(s) of our parish priest(s)?**

3. **How can we show our love for God at Mass?** (We can pray, sing, listen, and sit quietly.)

4. **How do we show we belong to God's family?** (We are kind to each other. We love one another as God loves us. We act as images of God.)

Extending the Lesson

Art and Craft Projects

Use these patterns from the special pattern packet.

B.

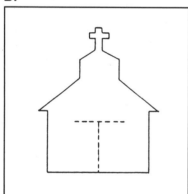

C.

Materials Needed

A. Half-pint milk cartons (one for each child), glue, lightweight paper, construction paper, crayons, scissors, stapler.

B. Church pattern, glue, scissors, pictures of people (cut from magazines).

C. Colored tissue paper, church window pattern, white construction paper, crayons, scissors.

A. Milk Carton Church. Cover the sides of a half-pint milk carton with lightweight white paper. Cut a square (4 by 4 inches) out of brown construction paper. Crease the square in the middle and staple it to the peak of the milk carton to form the roof. Cut a cross out of construction paper and glue or staple it to the roof. Have the children color windows and doors on their church. While the children are working on this project, remind them that the church is God's house on earth.

B. Construction Paper Church. Using the pattern provided, cut one church per child from construction paper. Cut along the dashed lines, as indicated on the pattern, to form the doors. Fold the doors open and have the children glue the church to another piece of construction paper. Cut pictures of a variety of people from magazines and glue these pictures behind the doors. Write on the bottom of their projects "We gather together in God's house to give thanks and praise." While the children are working on this project, remind them that all kinds of people belong to God's family—old, young, white, black, yellow, red, men, women, and so forth.

C. Church Window. Each child will need a church window pattern cut from construction paper. Cut a piece of tissue paper the same size as the pattern. Glue the church window pattern to the tissue paper. The children can color and decorate the window pattern. While the children are working on this project, remind them of the items we see in church and that these items are treated with respect because they are found in God's house.

Action Rhyme

> God's house is a special place, (*Fold fingers together, extend index fingers and thumbs to form a steeple.*)
> A place for you and me, (*Point to others and then to self.*)
> A place for everyone. (*Arms open wide.*)
> I always go to God's house (*Nod head "yes".*)
> To listen, learn, and pray. (*Point to ears, then to head, then fold hands.*)
> I show my love for God in a very special way. (*Hands on heart.*)

Prayer

> *Dear God, I will remember that Your house is special. I will treat it in a special way. Amen.*

Worksheets

The worksheets can be sent home to be completed or can be completed in the classroom and then sent home. In either case, the worksheets should be used as take-home material because they furnish the basis for parent–child faith discussion.

Pre-school A. Worksheet 12 can be distributed after the Living the Lesson section to help the children relate the theme to their daily lives. Worksheet 13 relates to the lesson theme and can be distributed to the children after the Application portion of the Lesson Presentation section to reinforce the concept.

Pre-school B. Worksheet 64 relates to the lesson theme and can be distributed to the children after the Application portion of the Lesson Presentation section to reinforce the concept. Worksheet 65 can be distributed after the Living the Lesson section to help the children relate the theme to their daily lives.

Kindergarten. Worksheets 16, 17 and 18 relate to the lesson theme and can be distributed to the children after the Application portion of the Lesson Presentation section to reinforce the concept.

Church Leaders

Lesson Focus

This lesson is an extension for kindergarten of Lesson 6, "God's House—The Church". The material is designed for one class period. Through this extension, the children gain a better understanding of the continuity of the Catholic Church. The authority given to Peter and the Apostles by Jesus was passed on by the Apostles and their successors to the Church leaders of today.

This lesson is an introduction to the hierarchy of the Church. The children will become familiar with the meaning of the words "Pope", "bishops", and "priests". The vocabulary words are:

Pope—the man who takes Peter's place and serves as head of the whole Catholic Church on earth today.

Bishops—the men who today teach the people and help them to be holy the way the Apostles did.

Priests—men who have answered God's call and have chosen to offer their lives to Him and act as helpers to the bishops.

Concepts of Faith

Who serves as the leader of the whole Catholic Church on earth?

The Pope serves as the leader of the whole Catholic Church on earth.

Lesson Presentation

Application

While presenting the following material to the children, you may wish to show pictures of Saint Peter, the Apostles, the Pope, the bishop of your diocese, and your parish priest(s) at the appropriate times.

When Jesus lived on earth, He chose twelve men to be His special helpers. These men were called the twelve Apostles. Jesus taught these men all about God. He showed them how an image of God acts. Jesus showed them how to live and how to love the way God does. Jesus asked these Apostles to go and teach all the people of the world. Jesus chose one of the Apostles to serve as the leader of the whole Catholic Church. Jesus chose Simon and changed his name to Peter, which mean "rock". Jesus told Peter, "Upon this rock I will build my Church" (Matt 16:18). Peter became the first Pope.

The Apostles taught many people about God. Soon other men wanted to help spread the word of God. Before the Apostles died, they placed their hands on the heads of these men to give them the gifts of understanding and of teaching God's word. They also received the gifts of offering Mass and of bringing the sacraments to the people. These men were called bishops. They taught the word of God after the Apostles died. The bishops helped the people to act as images of God.

The bishops could not go everywhere. They needed help. Other men came to the bishops. These men wanted to offer their lives to God in a certain way. The bishops blessed these men and made them priests. The priests helped the bishops by forgiving sins and offering Mass.

Today, Peter and the other Apostles are in heaven with God, but the Catholic Church goes on. As the years passed, other men were called by God and offered their lives to Him, becoming leaders of the Church: Pope, bishops, and priests. The name of our Pope today is _____. He is the leader of the whole Catholic Church on earth today. His leadership is a great service to us. He lives far away in the city of Rome.

The name of the bishop of our area is _____. He lives in _____. The priest(s) at our church is (are) Father _____. He (they) live(s) in our parish. All these men were called by God and have decided to be followers of Jesus in a certain way. The Pope leads the whole Church. The bishops teach God's word and help the people to be holy. The priests help the bishops by forgiving sins and offering Mass.

Discussion Questions

1. **Who began the Catholic Church?** (Jesus.)
2. **What do we call Jesus' first helpers?** (The Apostles.)
3. **How many Apostles were there?** (Twelve.)
4. **What did the Apostles do?** (They taught people about God and helped them to act as images of God.)
5. **Whom did Jesus choose as the first Pope?** (Peter.)

Living the Lesson

Jesus began the Catholic Church. We, as Catholics, believe what Jesus taught. The Church keeps on doing what Jesus did.

1. **What is the Pope's name?**
2. **What is our bishop's name?**
3. **What is (are) the name(s) of our parish priest(s)?**
4. **What do priests do?** (Priests forgive sins and offer Mass.)

Extending the Lesson

You may want to show pictures of the Vatican, telling the children that this is where the Pope lives. You may want to show the children pictures of the Pope and the bishop. Include a picture of the bishop wearing his miter and carrying a crosier.

Prayer

> *Dear God, please bless our Pope, bishops, and priests. Keep them in Your care. Help other men want to offer their lives to You as priests. Amen.*

Worksheet

The worksheet can be sent home to be completed or can be completed in the classroom and then sent home. In either case, the worksheet should be used as take-home material because it furnishes the basis for parent–child faith discussion.

Kindergarten. Worksheet 19 relates to the lesson theme and can be distributed to the children after the Application portion of the Lesson Presentation section to reinforce the concept.

Lesson 7   Wrong Choices—Sin

Workbook Pages

Pre-school A. 14–15
Pre-school B. 66–67
Kindergarten 20–21

Lesson Focus

Because we are all made in the image of God, we should all want to act like God. But because we are persons—that is, we have minds and wills—we can choose how to act. One effect of original sin is that it is difficult for our wills to exercise complete control over our bodies. This makes it hard, at times, to do what we know is right and to avoid what we know is wrong.

Even though most of the children are not of the age of reason and thus technically cannot sin, it is important to establish a sense of right and wrong. Along with this awareness of morality should come a sense of sorrow and a need for forgiveness when a wrong is committed.

Our vocabulary word, **sin**, can be explained as knowing something is wrong—knowing we are not supposed to do it—and doing it anyway. Sin is the opposite of love. When we sin, we hurt ourselves—not a hurt on the outside like a scraped knee or a cut finger, but a hurt on the inside. We also hurt (do not love) others, and we disobey (show a lack of love for) God. We are not even acting as persons, because a person is made in the image of God to do what God does, that is, love.

Concepts of Faith

How do we sin?

We sin by choosing to do something we know is wrong. We disobey God. We do not love Him as we should.

What happens when we sin?

When we sin, we hurt ourselves, we hurt others, and we displease God.

Lesson Presentation

Application

We have a choice in what we do. We can choose the right thing and be a bright reflection of God, or we can make the wrong choice. When we choose to do something we know is wrong, we dim our reflection of God.

Spray a light mist of water on the surface of a mirror. Sprinkle ash or dirt on the mirror so that it is smudged and dirty.

Begin by reminding the children of the presentation used in Lesson 3, showing that they are made in the image of God. Next, show the children the dirty mirror. Discuss how the image in the mirror is not clear. It is hard to see the image or what the image is doing. Explain that sometimes we do not reflect God clearly. When we choose to do something we know is wrong, we are not clear images of God. We have displeased God. This is called sin. Sin is the opposite of love. Just as dirt or ash dim our images in the mirror, wrong choices (sin) dim our reflection of God.

Discussion Questions

1. **Which mirror image should we want to be like, the clear one or the dim one?** (The clear one.)
2. **What is sin?** (Sin is choosing to do something we know is wrong. Sin is the opposite of love.)
3. **Whom do we hurt when we do something we know is wrong?** (God, others, and ourselves, because we are not acting as images of God.)
4. **Can we see the hurt of sin the way we can see a scrape on our knees or a cut on our fingers?** (No.)
5. **What did God give us to help us make the right choices?** (The Ten Commandments.)

Suggested Stories

A. "The Lady Who Made the Wrong Choice" (based on John 8:1–11)
B. "Adam and Eve Disobey God" (based on Genesis 3:1–24)

Living the Lesson

God gave us minds and wills so we can think and choose. If we always remember that we are made in the image of God, it will be easier for us to reflect God in our choices. When we choose to do something we know is wrong, we dim our reflection of God.

1. Discuss the difference between *choosing* to do something wrong—that is, doing it on purpose—and doing something wrong *by accident*. Doing something wrong on purpose is a sin, but accidents are not. List examples for the children and ask them which is an accident and which is a wrong choice:

   Spilling a glass of milk because your arm bumped it; spilling a glass of milk because you were playing instead of eating.

   Bumping into someone because it's very crowded; bumping into someone because you want to push them over.

2. **What should we do when we have chosen to do something wrong?** (Say that we are sorry to the person we have hurt or disobeyed, and say we are sorry to God. We ask God to help us not to do wrong again.)
3. **Is it always easy to make the right choices?** (No.)
4. Have the children pick the right (loving) choices:

   Tommy is hungry. Dinner will be ready soon. Tommy's mother said he could not have a cookie before dinner. Tommy's mother is in another room and cannot see Tommy. Should Tommy take a cookie?

Susie and her sister are not supposed to play ball in the house. Susie's parents are not home. Susie wants to play ball, and her sister wants to watch TV. Should Susie play ball in the house while her sister watches TV, or should she wait until the program is over and go outside?

More situations can be made up and discussed with the children.

Use these patterns from the special pattern packet.

A.

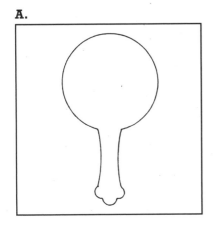

B.

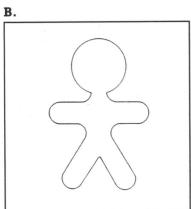

C.

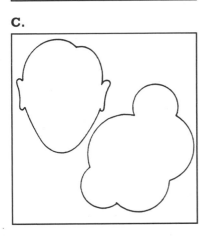

Extending the Lesson
Art and Craft Projects

Materials Needed
A. Construction paper, white tissue paper, foil, scissors, glue, stapler, mirror pattern provided for Lesson 3.
B. Paper doll pattern provided for Lesson 3, scissors, glue, stapler, construction paper, foil.
C. Cloudy image pattern, construction paper, scissors, brads.

A. "Image of God" Mirror. Glue a five- by three-inch piece of foil to a half sheet of construction paper. This will be like a small mirror. (Or use the mirror pattern provided for Lesson 3.) Cut a piece of white tissue paper the same size as the construction paper of the mirror pattern. Staple the tissue on top of the "mirror". Print on the bottom of the construction paper "Choosing to do something wrong dims our reflection of God." While the children are working, remind them that we dim our reflection of God when we disobey. Tell the children that, when we obey, we are loving God as we should. By saying and showing we are sorry, we will become bright images of God again.
B. "Image of God" Paper Doll. Using the paper doll pattern from Lesson 3, cut one paper doll per child. Have the children glue a round piece of foil to the face area. While they do this, remind the children that they are made in the image of God. Staple a round piece of tissue to the head of the paper doll. Remind the children of the mirror covered with dirt presented to them earlier. Explain that all we "think, and say, and do" should reflect God.
C. "Face and Cloud" Picture. Using the pattern of the face and cloud, cut both for each child. Have the children color the face to look like themselves. Connect the cloud to the top of the face with a brad so that the cloud can be slid over the face. Ask the children what happens when a cloud covers the sun. The cloud dims the sun's brightness. We see the sun less clearly. Explain that when we make wrong choices (sin), our reflection of God becomes clouded. We should try very hard to make right choices so we are bright images of God.

Action Rhyme

> When you know something is wrong (*Finger points to head.*)
> But do it anyway, you sin.
> You can't see it, (*Hands cover eyes.*)
> But it hurts you within. (*Hand on heart.*)
> Reach out for God, (*One hand raised up in the air.*)
> He'll give you a hand.
> But you must remember (*Finger on head.*)
> Not to do it again. (*Finger raised in warning.*)

Prayer

> *Dear God, I am sorry for all the things I have done that I knew were wrong. Please help me not to do them again. Amen.*

Worksheets

The worksheets can be sent home to be completed or can be completed in the classroom and then sent home. In either case, the worksheets should be used as take-home material because they furnish the basis for parent–child faith discussion.

Pre-school A. Worksheet 14 can be distributed after the Living the Lesson section to help the children relate the theme to their daily lives. Worksheet 15 can be used after the Suggested Story to aid the children's retention of the story.

Pre-school B. Worksheets 66 and 67 can be used after the Suggested Story to aid the children's retention of the story.

Kindergarten. Worksheet 20 relates to the lesson theme and can be distributed to the children after the Application portion of the Lesson Presentation section to reinforce the concept. Worksheet 21 can be distributed after the Living the Lesson section to help the children relate the theme to their daily lives.

The Lady Who Made the Wrong Choice

One day some people caught a lady doing something wrong. She was doing something she knew was very wrong, but she was doing it anyway. They decided on a very bad punishment for her. They decided to hurt her by throwing stones at her.

These people thought they could trick Jesus. They brought the lady who had done wrong to Jesus. The people knew that Jesus taught that those who were sorry for the wrong things they did should be forgiven. They were trying to see if Jesus really meant what He said about forgiving people.

But Jesus was not fooled. He knew they were trying to trick Him. Jesus said to the crowd, "The person who has never done a wrong thing can throw the first stone." No one moved; no one picked up a stone, not even a little pebble! All the people remembered something they had done that they knew was wrong. Slowly, they all walked away with their heads down. They all felt bad because they had tried to trick Jesus and because they wanted to hurt the lady instead of forgiving her and helping her to be good.

Jesus and the lady were left all alone. Jesus said to the lady, "Has no one found you guilty? I do not either. Now you can go back home. Remember to try hard to do the right thing."

No one is perfect. Everyone chooses to do something wrong sometimes. When we do something we know is wrong, we should say we are sorry to whomever we have hurt or disobeyed; we should say we are sorry to God; and we should make sure we ask God to help us never to do that wrong thing again.

Review Questions

1. **Why did people want to hurt the lady?** (She was doing something she knew was wrong.)
2. **What was the lady's punishment?** (The people were going to throw stones at her.)
3. **What did the people think Jesus would do?** (Forgive the lady.)
4. **Who did Jesus say should throw the first stone?** (The person who had never done anything wrong.)
5. **Did anyone throw a stone?** (No, because they all remembered something they had done that was wrong.)
6. **What did the people do then?** (They all went away feeling sorry.)
7. **What did Jesus say to the lady?** (Go home and do not do bad things anymore.)

Adam and Eve Disobey God

Adam and Eve were not like anything else God had made. They were persons like the angels. But Adam and Eve had bodies, and the angels did not. Adam and Eve were special because they were persons with bodies. They were made in the image of God. They could reflect God in all they "thought, and said, and did".

Adam and Eve lived in a beautiful garden called the Garden of Eden. The Garden was made by God because He loved Adam and Eve. God had given Adam and Eve everything they needed to live forever with Him. Together they shared food, water, sunshine, and happiness. But, best of all, they shared God's love with each other.

"You can eat from every tree in the Garden except from the tree of good and bad", said God. "If you eat from the tree of good and bad, you will not be able to live with Me forever."

Adam and Eve listened to God. They were happy in the Garden. They loved God, obeyed Him, and reflected Him in all they "thought, and said, and did", until one day when the devil spoke to Eve. The devil was not like Adam and Eve because he did not act as an image of God. He wanted to trick Eve.

"Is it true you can eat any of the fruit in the Garden?" the devil asked.

"No", Eve answered. "God said we should not eat from the tree of good and bad. If we eat from the tree of good and bad, we cannot live forever with God."

"But that is not true", the devil lied. "God only told you that because He does not want you to be as wise and powerful as He is."

Eve did not know the devil was lying. She did not know the devil was trying to trick her. Eve picked a fruit from the tree of good and bad. First she tasted the fruit, then she took the fruit to Adam.

Taste this fruit", she said. "It will make us as wise as God. It is the fruit from the tree of good and bad."

Adam tasted the fruit as Eve had asked. Suddenly, Adam and Eve felt ashamed. They knew they had done something wrong. They had not done as God had asked. They had not loved Him as they should have. They had disobeyed God.

Adam and Eve tried to hide from God, but God called to them. "Adam! Eve! Why are you hiding?" God asked.

"We know You will not be pleased with us", they said. "We have disobeyed You."

God knew what they had done. Adam and Eve had hurt the love they shared with God. Now they could not live with God forever.

God sent Adam and Eve away from the Garden. Now they would have to work very hard for all the things God had given them. They were not bright images of God. Adam and Eve had sinned. This sin of Adam's and Eve's was the first sin. We call it "original sin".

When we disobey God by choosing to do something we know is wrong, we do not love God as we should. We sin. Our reflection of God is not as bright as it had been. It is not always easy to make the right choices, but we should choose to act lovingly, like images of God, in all we "think, and say, and do".

Review Questions

1. **Where did Adam and Eve live?** (The Garden of Eden.)
2. **What did God tell them not to do?** (Eat from the tree of good and bad.)
3. **Who tricked Eve?** (The devil.)
4. **What happened when Adam and Eve disobeyed God?** (They had to leave the Garden.)

Lesson 8   God's Family—Baptism

Workbook Pages

Pre-school A. 16–17
Pre-school B. 68–69
Kindergarten 22–23

Lesson Focus

Baptism is the beginning and the foundation of our union with God. Through this sacrament, we become adopted sons and daughters and share in God's very own life. At Baptism, water is poured over our heads, signifying the cleansing of our souls from sin. Though we are never restored to the original state of creation, Baptism gives us grace that makes it possible for us to act as images of God, that is, to act in a fully human way. Not only does the newly baptized person celebrate, but the whole Catholic community celebrates this birth into God's family (the Church).

The vocabulary word is **grace**. Grace can be explained as a special gift of God's own life that makes us members of His family. Grace can be a difficult concept for the children to understand. Grace has two functions. First, grace makes us children of God; and second, grace strengthens our wills and makes it possible for us to act as images of God.

To illustrate the first function of grace, ask the children how they became members of their family. They were born into their family. When they were born to their moms and dads, the children became members of their family. The children share in the life of the family—they live with the family, share meals with the family. (For adopted children, you can point out that they were chosen by their moms and dads to become a part of their family.) This is similar to what grace does for us. We are given the gift of God's own life. We share in God's own life and therefore are members of His family.

To illustrate the second function, ask the children if any of them take vitamins. Vitamins help us grow in the right way. They help our bodies to be strong and help us stay healthy. Grace is similar to vitamins. Grace helps us act as images of God. Grace helps us to be strong and makes it possible for us to do the right thing. Our moms and dads give us vitamins because they love us and want us to be as healthy as we can be. God gives us grace because He loves us and wants us to be the best images of God we can be.

Concepts of Faith

Who are members of God's family?
All baptized people are members of God's family.

What is grace?
Grace is a share in God's own life.

Lesson Presentation

Application

Ask the children if any of them remember being present at the baptism of a younger brother or sister. Discuss with the children what they remember. (Who was at the baptism? What did the baby wear? What did they see? and so forth.)

To present this lesson we suggest that slides or pictures be taken at a baptism in the parish church. (You could have the children bring pictures of their baptisms, or you could bring pictures of a baptism, if taking slides or photos is not possible. We suggest that the pictures be taken at the parish church so the children become more familiar with their church.)

The following items should be included in the pictures presented to the children:

1. **Baptismal font:** The place in the church where the babies are baptized.

2. **Easter candle:** A special candle first lit on Easter and then used at all the baptisms. When the candle is lit, it reminds us that this is a time of prayer and that Jesus is the Light of our lives.

3. **The holy oils:** These oils are blessed by the bishop. The priest puts oil on his thumb and makes the "Sign of the Cross" on the baby's forehead and chest. Then the priest says prayers for the baby.

4. **The baby with parents and godparents:** The baby is brought to church by his parents and godparents. Godparents are special friends or relatives who promise to help the baby to learn about Jesus and, as the baby grows up, to live as an image of God.

5. **Water being poured on the baby:** Water that is blessed, called holy water, is used at baptisms. The holy water is poured over the baby's head. It looks as if the priest is washing the baby. That helps us remember that Baptism washes away original sin. The pouring of the water also helps us remember that God's life is coming into the child. As he pours the water, the priest says, "I baptize you in the name of the Father, and of the Son, and of the Holy Spirit", using the words we say when we make the "Sign of the Cross".

6. **The baby in a white garment:** The baby is wearing white clothes. The white clothes are very clean. They help us remember that original sin is gone, and God's life is in the baby.

7. **Parent or godparent holding a lighted candle:** A lighted candle is given to the baby's parents or godparents. The candle reminds us that Jesus is the Light of our lives. When the baby grows up and learns about Jesus, He will be the Light of the baby's life too.

8. **The priest touching the baby's ears and mouth:** The priest says many prayers for the baby. He touches the baby's ears and mouth. With our ears we can hear about Jesus, and with our mouths we can pray to Jesus. (Optional.)

9. **The priest blessing the family:** The priest makes the "Sign of the Cross", blessing the baby and everyone at the baptism. Now that the baby is baptized, the baby is free from original sin, is a living member of God's family, and someday could go to heaven.

Discussion Questions

1. **Are only babies baptized?** (No, sometimes older children and grownups are baptized because they were not baptized as babies.)
2. **Who should be baptized?** (Everyone.)
3. **What do we call the special gift of God's own life that we receive at Baptism?** (Grace.)
4. **Who are godparents?** (Special friends or relatives who promise to help us learn about Jesus and who set good examples for us.)
5. **Where do we go to be baptized?** (To church.)
6. **What does the priest pour over the baby's head?** (Holy water.)
7. **Are all baptized people members of God's family?** (Yes.)
8. **Do all baptized people have original sin washed away and do they receive God's life?** (Yes.)
9. **Could all members of God's family someday go to heaven?** (Yes.)

Suggested Stories

A. "John the Baptist" (based on Matthew 3:1–9)
B. "Jesus Is Baptized" (based on Matthew 3:13–17)

Living the Lesson

Through the sacrament of Baptism, we receive the gift of grace. Grace is God's own life. Grace makes it possible for us to act as images of God and makes us members of God's family. Therefore, grace helps us get to heaven.

1. Discuss the baptismal slides or pictures shown to the children. **What are some of the things seen at a baptism?** (Priest, baby, parents, godparents, candle, holy oils, and holy water.) **What color are the clothes the baby wears?** (White.) **Why are they white?** (To remind us that original sin is gone, and God's life is present.) **What does the priest pour over the baby's head?** (Holy water.) **What does it look as if the priest is doing?** (Pouring water and washing the baby.) **What does that help us remember?** (That Baptism washes away original sin and gives us God's life.)
2. **What do godparents do?** (Godparents promise to help us to learn about Jesus and to live as images of God.) Ask the children if they know who their godparents are.
3. **When we are baptized, whose family do we belong to?** (We become members of God's family. When we are baptized in the Catholic Church, we become Catholics.) Help the children find out in what church they were baptized.
4. **Does Baptism help us act as images of God so we can go to heaven someday?** (Yes.)

5. Using a ditto master or mimeograph stencil, make a copy of the following form for each child to take home and have filled out.

I became a member of God's family on _____ .
I was baptized at _____ church.
My godparents are _____ and _____ .

Extending the Lesson
Art and Craft Projects

Materials Needed
- **A.** Paper doll pattern, construction paper, scissors, glue.
- **B.** Construction paper, glue, scissors.
- **C.** Colored paper, scissors, glue.

Use this pattern from the special pattern packet.

A.

A. Paper Dolls. Using the pattern provided, cut six paper dolls (1 brown, 1 orange, 1 black, 1 yellow, 1 white, 1 red) per child. Glue the paper dolls hand-to-hand in a circle (the heads to the center). Write one word on each doll as follows: "We . . . all . . . belong . . . to . . . God's . . . family." As the children are working, remind them that through Baptism we become members of God's family.

B. Family Tree. Cut a tree trunk for each child from construction paper. Write "God" on the tree trunk and glue it to another piece of paper. Have the children tear pieces of different colored construction paper to be used as leaves. Have the children make one leaf for each member of their family. (They may choose to include godparents, grandparents, and so forth.) Write the names of the family members on the leaves and glue them on the tree. Write "We all belong to God's family" on the finished project. As the children are working, remind them that each of us has a family. But, through Baptism, each family is joined with many others in the family of God.

C. Flowers. Cut flowers from different colored paper. Use red, yellow, blue, and so forth. Glue the flowers on green construction paper to resemble a garden. As the children are working, remind them we all belong to God's family. Baptism joins us together even though we look different. Our differences make God's family beautiful.

Action Rhyme

I was baptized in the name of the Father— (*Touch forehead.*)
He made everyone; (*Point to self and others.*)
And I was baptized in the name of the Son— (*Touch your heart.*)
Jesus loves you and me; (*Point to self and others.*)
And I was baptized in the name of the Holy Spirit. (*Touch left shoulder and then right shoulder.*)
We're all God's family. (*Spread arms wide.*)

Prayer

> *Thank you, God, for welcoming me into Your family when I was baptized. Amen.*

Worksheets

The worksheets can be sent home to be completed or can be completed in the classroom and then sent home. In either case, the worksheets should be used as take-home material because they furnish the basis for parent–child faith discussion.

Pre-school A. Worksheet 16 can be distributed after the Living the Lesson section to help the children relate the theme to their daily lives. Worksheet 17 relates to the lesson theme and can be distributed to the children after the Application portion of the Lesson Presentation section to reinforce the concept.

Pre-school B. Worksheet 68 can be used after the Suggested Story to aid the children's retention of the story. Worksheet 69 relates to the lesson theme and can be distributed to the children after the Application portion of the Lesson Presentation section to reinforce the concept or after the Living the Lesson section to help the children relate the theme to their daily lives.

Kindergarten. Worksheet 22 relates to the lesson theme and can be distributed to the children after the Application portion of the Lesson Presentation section to reinforce the concept. Worksheet 23 can be used after its related Suggested Story to aid the children's retention of the story.

John the Baptist

Jesus had a cousin named John. John loved God very much. John had some very special work to do for God. John wanted to teach all the people about God. He wanted the people to ask God to forgive them for the wrong choices they had made. He wanted them to show God they were sorry for these wrong choices. "God will send someone more important than I", John told them. "He will show you the way to heaven, but you should be ready for His coming."

Then one day John asked the people to come into the river and be baptized. He wanted the people to show God that they were sorry for the wrong choices they had made. The people were showing God that they were sorry for their sins and that they wanted God to wash their sins away. They promised God to try not to sin again.

Soon many people were asking John to baptize them. One by one John baptized them. "Go now and live good lives", John would tell them.

After a while, People began to call John "the Baptist". The people listened to John because they wanted to learn more about God.

The baptisms John did were not the same as the baptisms the priests do now, because John was not a priest and the words he used were different.

Review Questions

1. **What special work did John do?** (He taught the people about God and baptized them.)
2. **Who was John?** (Jesus' cousin.)
3. **What did John ask the people to do after they were baptized?** (Go and live good lives.)
4. **What did the people call John?** (John the Baptist.)
5. **Did John do the same kind of baptisms that the priest does today?** (No, because John was not a priest and the words he used were different.)

Jesus Is Baptized

Long ago there lived a man called John. He was a cousin of Jesus. John told the people to show their love for God by changing their lives. "Come into the water and be baptized", he said. "Show God you want to start a new life."

One day, while John was baptizing people in the river, he saw Jesus standing before him. John was very surprised to see Jesus. "Why have You come to me?" he asked. "I am not important enough to baptize You. You should be baptizing me."

But Jesus answered, "I want to do what God the Father wants. I want to be baptized."

John did as Jesus had asked. As John baptized Jesus, a dove appeared over Jesus' head. The dove was a sign of God the Holy Spirit. Then God the Father's voice was heard: "This is my Son. I love Him. He has pleased Me."

John knew the dove was a sign of God the Holy Spirit. John knew he had pleased God.

When we are baptized by a priest, more happens to us than happened to the people John baptized. We become members of God's family, original sin is washed away, and we receive the gift of grace, a sharing in God's life. Grace makes it possible for us to live as images of God and helps us get to heaven. By being baptized, Jesus wanted to show us that all people are to be baptized.

Review Questions

1. **Why did John want people to be baptized?** (To start new lives.)
2. **Who surprised John by asking to be baptized?** (Jesus.)
3. **What appeared over Jesus' head?** (A dove, a symbol of the Holy Spirit.)
4. **What happens to us when we are baptized?** (We become members of God's family, and we receive the gift of grace.)
5. **Why was Jesus baptized?** (To show us that all people are to be baptized.)

Lesson 9   **Forgiveness Is an Act of Love**

Workbook Pages
Pre-school A. 18–19
Pre-school B. 70–71
Kindergarten 24–26

Lesson Focus

It is important that the children understand that we all make wrong choices, sometimes causing hurt or unhappiness to others. This does not mean we are bad persons, but rather that the deed is wrong and unacceptable to God. When we have done wrong, it does not mean that God and the person we have offended no longer love us, but rather we have hurt them and need to ask for forgiveness.

It should be emphasized that saying "I'm sorry" is only half of asking for forgiveness. We must also show through our action that we are truly sorry and will try to do better. Further, we must forgive others as God forgives us. The loving forgiveness we extend to each other is a sign of God's love.

The vocabulary word is **forgive**. To forgive is an act of love. We do not remind others when they have hurt us, but we keep on loving them. We show we have forgiven someone by a hug, a smile, or a kind word. We must remember that God forgives us when we are truly sorry and ask for His forgiveness. We are acting as images of God when we forgive others as God forgives us.

Concepts of Faith

Whom do we ask to forgive us when we do something wrong?
When we do something wrong, we ask God and the person we have hurt or disobeyed to forgive us.

How should we forgive others?
We should forgive others as God forgives us.

Lesson Presentation

Application

Prepare a mirror smeared with dirt or ash as in Lesson 7. Remind the children of the effect of sin, that is, hurting ourselves by dimming our reflection of God, displeasing God, and hurting others. Slowly begin to clear the mirror, leaving it somewhat smeared. Tell the children that when we say we are sorry for a wrong choice, our reflection of God begins to clear. But it is not enough to say "I'm sorry." Our actions and attitudes must also show we are sorry. We must try not to do the wrong again. Clean the mirror completely. Tell the children that both actions and words are needed to show we are truly sorry.

When we forgive others, we must also forget what they have done and not remind them of their wrong choices. We want to forgive others as God forgives us.

Discussion Questions

1. **Do we all do things that are wrong sometimes?** (Yes.)
2. **Do we need to ask forgiveness?** (Yes.)
3. **Does God forgive us?** (Yes.)
4. **Does God want us to forgive others?** (Yes.)
5. **How do we ask for forgiveness?** (We say "I'm sorry" to the person we have hurt and to God, and we try not to do wrong again.)
6. **How do we forgive others?** (We forgive others as God forgives us.)

Suggested Stories

A. "The Prodigal Son" (based on Luke 15:11–32)
B. "The Man Who Did Not Forgive" (based on Matthew 18:21–35)

Living the Lesson

We must learn to forgive others as God forgives us. We share God's forgiving love with others. Through our acts of forgiveness, we act as images of God.

1. **Ask the children to name some actions that show forgiveness.** (Hugs, kisses, handshakes, pats on the head, kind words, and so forth.)
2. **How do you feel when someone hurts you?** (Sad, angry, and so forth.)
3. **How do you feel when you hurt someone else?** (Embarrassed, unhappy, and so forth.)
4. **How does forgiving someone and being forgiven make us feel?** (Safe, loved, happy, and so forth.)
5. **List some situations when we should forgive others.** (When someone hits us, when someone does not want to play with us, when someone calls us names, and so forth.)
6. **Whom do we ask to forgive us when we have done wrong?** (God and those we have hurt or disobeyed.)
7. **Is it easy to say we were wrong and to ask for forgiveness?** (No.)

Extending the Lesson

Art and Craft Projects

Materials Needed

A. Lunch bags, construction paper, glue, scissors, pattern pieces provided.

B. Forgiving arms pattern, picture of each child (optional), glue, scissors, crayons.

C. Construction paper, glue, pencil, crayons.

Use these patterns from the special pattern packet.

A.

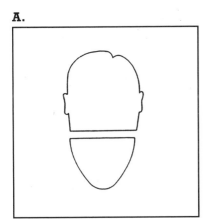

B.

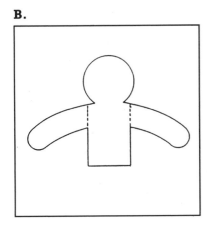

A. "Prodigal Son" Puppet. Give each child a brown lunch-size bag. Cut all the parts of the puppet from construction paper, using the pattern provided. With the bag folded flat, glue pattern piece **A**, the top of the head, on the bottom of the bag. Glue pattern piece **B**, the bottom of the head, to the bottom of the bag, sliding it under the fold on the bottom of the bag. Have the children draw the facial features on the prodigal son puppet. By sliding one hand inside the bag and manipulating the flap, the child can open and close the puppet's mouth. The children may act out the prodigal son story or may act out situations that happen at home and school and that require forgiveness.

B. "Forgiving Arms". Cut a pair of folding arms for each child from the pattern provided. Have the children draw a picture of themselves (or glue a photo of themselves, or cut and glue pictures of children from a magazine) in the middle of the folding arms. Write the words "Forgiveness is an act of love" on the folding arms. Remind the children that God forgives us when we say and show we are truly sorry. We should forgive others as God forgives us.

C. "Heart and Hands" Picture. Have the children cut a heart from red construction paper. Glue the heart in the middle of another piece of construction paper. Have the children take turns tracing their hands on either side of the heart. Label the picture "Forgiveness is an act of love." Remind the children that it is not always easy to forgive, and it is not always easy to ask for forgiveness. When we act as images of God, we forgive others as God forgives us.

Action Rhyme

I try to be good, (*Nod head "yes".*)
And always obey,
And when I do wrong, (*Shake head "no".*)
I remember to say, (*Point to mouth.*)
"I'm sorry, dear God, (*Hands folded in prayer.*)
"Please guide me each day,
"Help me forgive others at school, work, and play."

Prayer

Forgive me, heavenly Father, for my wrong choices. Help me be forgiving and loving to all people. Amen.

Worksheets

The worksheets can be sent home to be completed or can be completed in the classroom and then sent home. In either case, the worksheets should be used as take-home material because they furnish the basis for parent–child faith discussion.

Pre-school A. Worksheet 18 relates to the lesson theme and can be distributed to the children after the Application portion of the Lesson Presentation section to reinforce the concept. Worksheet 19 may be used after the Suggested Story to aid the children's retention of the story.

Pre-school B. Worksheet 70 can be distributed after the Living the Lesson section to help the children relate the theme to their daily lives. Worksheet 71 relates to the lesson theme and can be distributed to the children after the Application portion of the Lesson Presentation section to reinforce the concept.

Kindergarten. Worksheet 24 can be used after the Suggested Story to aid the children's retention of the story. Worksheet 25 can be distributed after the Living the Lesson section to help the children relate the theme to their daily lives. Worksheet 26 can be distributed after the vocabulary word is introduced.

Prodigal Son

Once there was a boy named Tom. He lived on a farm with his older brother, his mother, and his father. Tom was tired of living on the farm. He was tired of listening to his father and doing what he was told.

"I think I would be happier if I could go away from here", Tom said to himself. "Then I could do as I please."

Tom went to tell his father that he was going to leave. Tom did not think about how much he would hurt his father by leaving.

"Give me the money you promised so I can find my own happiness", Tom told his father. Then off Tom went with his money.

Everything seemed so wonderful. Tom could buy anything he wanted and do anything he liked. He made many new friends. But soon Tom had spent all his money. He had no money to do things with his friends. So they had no time to spend with Tom.

Tom knew he must get a job, but no one seemed to need him. Then, one day, a farmer said, "Come home with me. I need someone to take care of my pigs."

Tom was cold, hungry, and sad. All he had to eat was the food he fed the pigs. He missed his father and his nice home.

"Oh, how foolish I've been", Tom said. "I have wasted the money my father saved for me. I have only animal food to eat. I thought only about myself. I have hurt myself. Maybe I have hurt my father by leaving him. He needed my help, but I did not want to stay with him."

Tom knew his father loved him. Now Tom knew just how much he loved his father. The very next morning, he started home. As Tom walked up the driveway, he could see his father.

"Father", Tom called. "I'm so sorry I have hurt you. Please forgive me. I will do anything for you. You do not even have to call me 'son'. I'll work for you like a hired hand. You treat your workers better than I've been treated."

Tom's father gave him a big bear hug. "I have missed you very much. I forgive you, and I love you, my son", said Tom's father.

Tom's father was so excited to have Tom back that he called all his friends and gave a party.

"My son was lost", he said, "but now he has found his way home."

When we make wrong choices, we move away from God the way Tom moved away from his father. We should ask God to forgive us, show we are sorry, and try not to do wrong again. God's forgiveness is a sign of His great love. We should forgive others as God forgives us.

Review Questions

1. **Did Tom think he would hurt his father by leaving home?** (No.) **Did he hurt his father?** (Yes.)
2. **How did Tom feel after leaving home and wasting all his money?** (Very sad and foolish.)
3. **Where did Tom get a job?** (With a farmer, feeding his pigs.)
4. **What did Tom say to his father when he got back home?** ("I'm sorry. You don't have to call me 'son'.")
5. **What did Tom's father tell him?** (I forgive you, and I love you.)
6. **How did Tom's father act as an image of God?** (By forgiving Tom as God forgives us.)

The Man Who Did Not Forgive

Long ago there lived a man who owed money to the king. He owed the king a large amount of money, maybe more than a million dollars. This man owed so much money that the king said, "I will sell your home and all your furniture. Even then you will still owe me money!"

The man was very sorry he owed the king so much money. He fell down on the ground at the king's feet and begged, "Oh, kind king, please be patient with me. I am sorry I have not paid you the money. Please give me more time, and I will pay you all that I owe you."

The king felt sorry for the man and said, "Very well, I forgive you. I will forget all about the money you owe me. Go home. You owe me nothing."

The man left the king and went straight to the home of someone who owed him just a few dollars. The man demanded, "Give me what you owe me now!"

The poor man cried, "Please give me a little more time, and I will pay you." But the first man would not forgive him. The poor man had to sell his things to pay what he owed.

When the king heard what the first man had done, the king was very upset! He said to the man, "Remember how I forgave what you owed me? It was a very large amount, but I felt sorry for you and forgave you. But you did not forgive others." Then the king made the man sell all his things until he could pay all that he owed.

When we ask, God forgives us, because He loves us very much. To act as images of God, we need to forgive others as God forgives us.

Review Questions

1. **How much did the man owe the king?** (A large amount.)
2. **What was the king going to do to get his money?** (Sell the man's house and all his furniture.)
3. **Did the king forgive the man?** (Yes.)
4. **How much did the second man owe?** (A little amount.)
5. **Did the first man forgive the second man?** (No.)
6. **Why was the king upset?** (Because the king forgave the first man, and the first man did not forgive the other man.)
7. **How are we to forgive others?** (We are to forgive others as God forgives us.)

Lesson 10 **Prayer**

Lesson Focus

In prayer we think and reflect about our relationship with God. When we pray, we talk to God and are joined with Him and all His family, past and present.

We can pray privately or join with others, for example, at Mass. For Jesus said, "Where two or more are gathered in my name, there I am in their midst" (Matt 18:20).

It should be emphasized that God hears all prayers—our silent thoughts and our spoken words—because He is with us always. We can thank Him for all He has given us, ask for assistance and forgiveness, or sing His praises.

The vocabulary word is **prayer**—talking to God quietly or out loud, alone or with others.

Concepts of Faith

What is prayer?

Prayer is talking to God quietly or out loud, alone or with others. We can say "thank you", ask for help, say "I'm sorry", and sing God's praises.

Lesson Presentation

Application

Ask the children if they talk to their friends. If they had a friend, but they never talked to this friend, what would happen? They would not be friends very long! We talk to our friends every day. We miss our friends when we do not talk to them. This is what prayer is like. God loves us very much. So much that He made us in His image. We should talk to God often, asking Him to help us act as images of God.

Tell the children that today they will be learning a special prayer—a prayer that Jesus taught His special friends, the Apostles. This prayer is called the "Our Father". We call God our Father because He made us in His image. We are His children. When we pray, we first praise God for all His goodness and love. We begin this prayer by saying, "Our Father, who art in heaven, hallowed by Thy name." When we say these words, we mean "our Father in heaven, Your name is holy."

Then we should tell God that we will try to act as images of God. We say, "Thy kingdom come; Thy will be done on earth as it is in heaven." That means we will try to do what God wants us to here on earth, just as the angels and saints do what God wants in heaven.

Next, we ask God for our daily food by saying "Give us this day our daily bread." When we say this, we are not just asking for bread and other food for our bodies, but we are asking for ways to learn more about God in all we "think, and say, and do". Then we say, "and forgive us our trespasses as we forgive those who trespass against us." This means we are to forgive people who do wrong, just as God forgives us when we do wrong and are sorry.

We end by saying "and lead us not into temptation, but deliver us from evil." Here we ask for God's help so we can always act as images of God and reflect God in all we "think, and say, and do".

Jesus taught the Apostles this special prayer to help them and us know how to pray. Since we say the "Our Father" during Mass, you have already heard it.

Have the children stand and repeat the "Our Father", phrase by phrase, after you.

The "Our Father" can now be included in the children's daily prayers. You may wish to have them repeat each phrase after you until they are more familiar with the words.

Discussion Questions

1. **What is prayer?** (Prayer is talking to God quietly or out loud, alone or with others.)
2. **What can we say when we pray?** (We can say "thank you", ask for help, say I'm sorry", or sing God's praises.)
3. **Who taught us how to pray?** (Jesus.)
4. **What is the name of the special prayer Jesus taught?** (The "Our Father".)
5. **What does "hallowed be Thy name" mean?** (God's name is holy.)
6. **When we say "give us this day our daily bread", does that mean we are asking for just food to eat?** (No, it means we are asking for ways to learn about God and for the help to act as images of God in all we "think, and say, and do".)
7. **When is one of the times we pray the "Our Father" together with others?** (At Mass.)

Suggested Stories

A. "Jesus Teaches Us to Pray" (based on Luke 11:1–4)
B. "The Pharisee and the Tax Collector" (based on Luke 18:9–14)

Living the Lesson

Jesus prayed often and taught others how to pray. Jesus wants us to follow His example and pray often to our Father in heaven. Remind the children that God hears all our prayers, even when we do not say the words out loud. Sometimes we do not get what we pray for because God knows what is best for us.

1. **Whom are we talking to when we pray?** (God.)
2. **Does God always hear our prayers?** (Yes.)
3. **How often should we pray?** (Every day.)

4. **Give some examples of times we pray.** (Before and after meals, in the morning when we get up, before we go to bed, when we are sad, when we are scared, when we are sick, and so forth.)
5. **Do we pray only in church?** (No, we can pray anywhere, because God is with us always.)
6. Have the children list things they would like to pray for. Include these petitions in the children's daily prayers at school.

Extending the Lesson

Art and Craft Projects

Materials Needed

A. Construction paper, yarn, hole punch, crayons, "Our Father" workbook pages.

B. Construction paper, hole punch, yarn, stapler, pattern pieces provided.

A. "Our Father" Booklet. Tear the pages of the "Our Father" booklet from the children's workbook. Hand these out to the children. Have the children color each page, using crayons. Give the children a piece of construction paper so they can design a cover. Three-hole punch the booklet pages and the cover. Have the children lace yarn through the holes in the pages and tie the yarn to form a booklet. Lead the children through the prayer again, reminding them of what the words mean. Tell the children to listen for the "Our Father" when they go to Mass.

B. Prayer Mobile. Using the patterns provided, cut the pieces for the prayer mobile from construction paper for each child. Write "I pray to God with love" across the rainbow. Punch a hole at the top of each piece. Hang the items on pieces of yarn from the rainbow. Staple a loop at the top of the rainbow so it can be hung. Explain the symbols to the children: The Bible is a book with stories about God and Jesus' life on earth. Our hearts are full of love for God. We tell God of our love for him in our prayers. The cross reminds us that Jesus loved us so much He died for us. The hands remind us how to pray. God hears all our prayers—our silent thoughts and our spoken words.

Use this pattern from the special pattern packet.

B.

Action Rhyme

Sometime we pray quietly, (*Bow head, fold hands.*)
Sometimes we pray out loud, (*Cup hands around mouth.*)
Sometimes we pray alone or in a crowd. (*Hug self, then spread arms wide.*)
Sometimes we sing His praises, (*Arms above head.*)
Say "thanks", "I'm sorry", or "please help me", (*Reach hand out.*)
God will always hear us, (*Point to heaven.*)
And near us He will be. (*Arms spread wide.*)

Prayer

> *Dear God, help us remember You always hear our prayers. Teach us how to pray. Amen.*

Worksheets

The worksheets can be sent home to be completed or can be completed in the classroom and then sent home. In either case, the worksheets should be used as take-home material because they furnish the basis for parent–child faith discussion.

Pre-school A. Worksheets 20–22 can be used (1) as suggested in Option A of the Art and Craft Projects portion of the Extending the Lesson section, or (2) after the Application portion of the Lesson Presentation section to reinforce the concept, or (3) after the Suggested Story to aid the children's retention of the story.

Pre-school B. Worksheets 72–74 can be used (1) as suggested in Option A of the Art and Craft Projects portion of the Extending the Lesson section, or (2) after the Application portion of the Lesson Presentation section to reinforce the concept.

Kindergarten. Worksheets 27–29 can be used (1) as suggested in Option A of the Art and Craft Projects portion of the Extending the Lesson section, or (2) after the Application portion of the Lesson Presentation section to reinforce the concept, or (3) after its related Suggested Story to aid the children's retention of the story. Worksheets 30 and 31 can be distributed after the Living the Lesson section to help the children relate the theme to their daily lives.

Jesus Teaches Us to Pray

When Jesus lived on earth, He often went off by Himself to pray. One day, His special friends, the Apostles, asked Jesus to teach them to pray, too.

Jesus told them to pray something like this: Our Father, who art in heaven, hallowed be Thy name, Thy kingdom come; Thy will be done on earth as it is in heaven. Give us this day our daily bread and forgive us our trespasses as we forgive those who trespass against us; and lead us not into temptation, but deliver us from evil. Amen.

Jesus told his friends it is important to pray every day. He told them that God hears all our prayers. God knows what is best for us and gives us all we need to be happy on earth and to reach heaven.

Review Questions

1. **Did Jesus pray when He lived on earth?** (Yes, often.)
2. **Who asked Jesus to teach them how to pray?** (The Apostles.)
3. **What prayer did Jesus teach them?** (The "Our Father".)
4. **Should we pray often?** (Yes, every day.)
5. **Does God hear all our prayers?** (Yes.)
6. **Do we always get what we pray for?** (No, God knows what is best for us.)

The Pharisee and the Tax Collector

One day, Jesus told a story about two men who went to the temple to pray. One man was called a Pharisee. He kept all the rules completely, no matter what. He was more concerned about rules than about really loving God. The other man was a tax collector. No one liked him very much.

Both men went to the temple to pray. The Pharisee walked proudly to the front of the temple. He made sure everyone saw him. He felt very important. The Pharisee began to pray very loudly, "I'm so glad I'm not like other people. I never make wrong choices. I always follow all the rules and tell others when they are not following them." On and on he prayed, bragging and boasting about himself and pointing out what others did wrong.

The tax collector, however, stood quietly. He did not even raise his eyes toward heaven. The tax collector bowed his head and said, "Dear God, forgive me. Sometimes I make wrong choices. I'm truly sorry."

Jesus told the people that they should act like the tax collector when they pray. God knows what you have done. Do not brag about the good things you do or feel important because you help others. You please God by thanking Him for all He has given you. Tell God you love Him. Ask Him to help and guide you to be the best image of God you can be. If you have made wrong choices, tell God you are sorry. Ask Him to help you not to do wrong again.

When Jesus finished talking to the people, they knew how to pray. They knew that when they prayed they could say "thank you", ask for help, say "I'm sorry", and praise God.

Review Questions

1. **How did the Pharisee act when he prayed?** (He bragged and boasted. He never thanked God or told God he loved Him.)
2. **How did the tax collector pray?** (Quietly he offered God his love and asked for forgiveness.)
3. **What should we do when we pray?** (Give thanks, ask for help, ask for forgiveness, say "I love you", and praise God.)

Lesson Focus

This is an extension for kindergarten of the lesson "Prayer". The material is designed for one class period. When you present this lesson, you introduce the children to the Mass as the perfect prayer.

The Mass is offered to God to worship Him, to thank Him, to say we are sorry for our sins, and to ask for help. It is the sacrifice of Jesus on the Cross, offered in our church by the priest. As the family of God, we listen carefully at Mass, say the prayers, and sing the songs.

The vocabulary word is **Mass**. The Mass is the perfect prayer. At Mass stories about God are read, and God gives us the gift of Himself at Communion. At Mass we love God, and God loves us.

Concepts of Faith

What is Mass?

Mass is the most perfect prayer. At Mass stories about God are read, and God gives us the gift of Himself at Communion. At Mass we love God, and God loves us.

Lesson Presentation

Application

Using the pictures of the Mass from the children's workbook, review the various parts of the Mass. Begin by explaining to the children that there are many parts to the Mass.

1. Entrance

(Hold up picture of priest and altar boys processing to altar.)

As the priest and the altar boys walk to the altar, the people stand and often sing a song. The priest and the people start the Mass by making the "Sign of the Cross". When the "Sign of the Cross" is made, we are saying we believe in God, and we are offering this Mass to Him as a sign of our love.

2. Priest at the pulpit

(Hold up corresponding picture.)

We stand and listen to the priest as he reads us a story about Jesus' life on earth. When the priest has finished reading, he teaches us how to act as images of God.

3. Offertory

(Picture of people bringing up gifts.)

As some people carry the special gifts of bread and wine to the priest, we should offer ourselves in love as a gift to God.

Tell the children that the next part of the Mass is the most important. We call it the Consecration. During the Consecration, the priest changes the bread and wine into the Body and Blood of Jesus.

4. Elevation of the Host and elevation of the chalice
(Show both pictures at the same time.)

Even though the bread and wine have not changed on the outside, even though they *look* the same, they really *are* changed. The priest holds up the Body and Blood of Christ in the form of bread and wine. (If your parish rings bells at the Consecration, tell the children that the bells are rung to remind us that Jesus is with us in a very special way.) When the priest holds up the Host and the chalice for us to see, we should whisper, "Jesus, I love You." Jesus gives His Body and Blood to us because He loves us.

After this, we pray together as God's family the prayer Jesus taught us, the "Our Father". We should say the "Our Father" with the priest and all God's family at Mass.

5. Sign of peace
(Picture of priest and altar boys shaking hands.)

Jesus shared a sign of peace with His friends as an act of His love. We share a sign of peace with others at Mass as an act of love too. We shake the hands of those near us and say, "Peace be with you."

6. Communion
(Picture of people receiving Communion.)

Jesus loves us by giving us the gift of Himself at Communion. Tell the children that at this time they should sit quietly and say a prayer to Jesus. Soon they, too, will be old enough to receive Jesus in this special way.

7. Final blessing
(Picture of priest blessing the people.)

The priest blesses us as he makes the "Sign of the Cross". We should make the "Sign of the Cross", too. As the priest and altar boys leave the altar, we usually join together in song.

Discussion Questions

1. **Who offers the Mass for us?** (The priest.)
2. **How do we begin and end our prayer?** (With the "Sign of the Cross".)
3. **How do we begin and end the Mass, the perfect prayer?** (With the "Sign of the Cross".)
4. **What happens at the most important part of the Mass?** (The bread and wine are changed into Jesus.)
5. **What is the prayer we say together as God's family?** (The "Our Father".)
6. **What is the special gift Jesus gives us at Communion?** (Himself.)

Suggested Story

"The Stranger on the Road" (based on Luke 24:13–35)

Living the Lesson

At Mass, God's family gathers to worship in the perfect prayer.

1. **Are you too little to follow along at Mass?** (No.)
2. **How can we share in the Mass?** (By making the "Sign of the Cross", listening to the stories, offering ourselves to God, telling Jesus we love Him, saying the "Our Father", sharing a sign of peace, singing the songs, and so forth.)
3. **How do we behave at Mass?** (We sit quietly so we can pray and so we do not disturb others.)

Extending the Lesson

Art and Craft Project

Materials Needed
Workbook pages, scissors, brads, hole punch.

Remove the pages on the Mass from the children's workbook. Cut along the broken lines to separate the pages. Punch two holes, one at the top and one at the bottom, on the left side of the pages. Placing the pages in the proper order, secure with brads. The children may choose to color the pictures. Tell them they can take their books to church to help them remember what they have learned about the Mass.

Prayer

> *Dear God, when I go to Mass, help me remember You are there in a special way. Thank You for this perfect prayer, the Mass. Amen.*

Worksheets

The worksheets can be sent home to be completed or can be completed in the classroom and then sent home. In either case, the worksheets should be used as take-home material because they furnish the basis for parent–child faith discussion.

Kindergarten. Worksheets 32–35 can be distributed to the children after the Application portion of the Lesson Presentation section to reinforce the concept or can be used as suggested in the Art and Craft Project portion of the Extending the Lesson section.

The Stranger on the Road

On the first Easter Sunday, two friends of Jesus were walking along the road to a village called Emmaus. As the two men walked, they talked about all the things that had happened to Jesus during the past three days. While they were talking, a man came up and started to walk with them. "What are you talking about?" asked the stranger. The two men were very surprised.

"You must be the only person in town who does not know what happened these last three days", one friend said.

"What happened?" asked the stranger.

The two friends began to tell the stranger all that had happened to Jesus. They told him how some men, who did not like Jesus or believe what He taught, wanted to hurt Jesus so that the people would stop believing in Him. These men had come with a group of people and had taken Jesus away. Jesus' two friends told the stranger about how Jesus had been tied up and hurt. They told the stranger how the people made Jesus carry a wooden cross. They told the stranger how, finally, these people had nailed Jesus to the cross and how He had died.

Then the second friend said, "Today some of the women who were friends of ours decided to bring flowers to Jesus' grave. When they got to the grave, they did not find Jesus. Instead, two angels asked why they were looking for Jesus in a grave. The angels told the women that Jesus had risen from the dead!"

The stranger then began to talk to the two friends about the things Jesus had taught them and about what the Scriptures said about Jesus. They two friends enjoyed listening and talking with the stranger so much that, when they reached the village, they asked the stranger to have dinner with them. The stranger stayed with them.

When they all sat down to eat, the stranger took bread, blessed it, and gave it to the men. Suddenly, Jesus' two friends realized who the stranger was! It was their friend Jesus. He had really risen! Just when they recognized Jesus, He disappeared from their sight.

The two friends hurried all the way back to the city! They wanted to tell the Apostles and the rest of Jesus' friends what had happened. When they reached the Apostles, the two friends told their story—how they talked to a stranger and how they recognized Jesus when He blessed the bread and gave it to them. They shared the wonderful news that Jesus truly had risen!

Jesus blessed bread and gave it to His friends to show them that He loved them and was still with them. When we go to Mass, we know that Jesus loves us and is with us in a special way, too. Jesus loves us by giving us the gift of Himself at Communion.

Review Questions

1. **Who joined Jesus' friends as they walked along the road?** (A stranger.)
2. **What did the two friends tell the stranger?** (All that had happened to Jesus during the past three days.)
3. **What did Jesus' friends ask the stranger to do?** (Have dinner with them.)
4. **Who was the stranger?** (Jesus.)
5. **When did the two friends recognize Jesus?** (When He took the bread, blessed it, and gave it to them.)
6. **When does Jesus give us the special gift of Himself?** (At Mass during Communion.)

Lesson 11 **Jesus Is God the Son**

Workbook Pages
Pre-school A. 23–24
Pre-school B. 75–76
Kindergarten 36–38

Lesson Focus

We are created in the image of God to do as He does, that is, to love. Unless we know God, we do not know ourselves. God revealed Himself to us first through creation and then through the second Person of the Blessed Trinity, Jesus. In the Old Testament, God told us about Himself, but in the New Testament, through Jesus, God shows Himself. Jesus said, "Whoever has seen me has seen the Father" (John 14:9).

Jesus is the One whose coming was foretold in the Scriptures. He came down from heaven to save us from our sins, that is, to redeem us. Thus, He shows us who we are and makes it possible for us to live as images of God now and to be happy forever with God in heaven.

Sometimes children are confused about Who Jesus is. It is essential that they understand that Jesus is God the Son. He is the second Person of the Blessed Trinity.

Scripture is the vocabulary word. It can be explained as the holy writings about God. Today we read stories about God in the Bible.

Concepts of Faith

Who is Jesus?
Jesus is God the Son.

Lesson Presentation

Application

Show the children a picture of a scroll. Explain to the children that a scroll is like a book. When Jesus was on earth, He read from scrolls. Jesus read the holy writings about God that were on the scrolls. We do not use scrolls today. We have books. What is the name of the book that tells us about God and tells us stories about Jesus' life on earth? (The Bible.)

Have different kinds of Bibles available, such as a children's picture Bible, a paperback Bible, and a fancy family Bible. Show the children different kinds of Bibles. Tell them that some Bibles are written for children. Those Bibles have lots of pictures and few words. Other Bibles are for families. There is a place in some Bibles to write down all the names of the people in the family. These Bibles have lots of words and a few pictures. Still other Bibles are for grownups. They have all words and no pictures.

Tell the children there are two main parts to the Bible. The first part is called the Old Testament. The Old Testament tells us about God and about us. It tells us about Someone whom God would send to show us who we are and how to live. This Someone would also make it possible for us to live as images of God. (Ask the children Who that Someone was that God sent to us. They should answer "Jesus".)

The second part of the Bible is called the New Testament. In the New Testament we read stories about Jesus' life on earth. Jesus' friends wrote the first stories about Him a very long time ago. They wrote these stories in a language different from the one we speak. Jesus' friends wrote in a language called Greek. Ask the children how they think we still have these stories today, if they were written so long ago and in a different language. Tell them that people read the stories that were written in this language, and then the people rewrote them in many other languages, and English was one of these languages.

Discussion Questions

1. **What is a scroll?** (A scroll is like a book.)
2. **Do we read scrolls today?** (No, we have books.)
3. **What do we call the book that tells us about God and tells us stories about Jesus' life on earth?** (The Bible.)
4. **What are the two main parts of the Bible?** (The Old Testament and the New Testament.)
5. **Whom does the Old Testament tell us about?** (God and us.)
6. **Whom does the New Testament tell stories about?** (Jesus and us.)
7. **Who is Jesus?** (Jesus is God the Son, the second Person of the Blessed Trinity.)

Suggested Stories

A. "Jesus Reads the Scriptures" (based on Luke 4:14–30)
B. "The Woman at the Well" (based on John 4:4–30)

Living the Lesson

We believe that Jesus is God the Son because the Church teaches us that in the Bible Jesus told the people that He was God the Son. We believe that Jesus, God the Son, became man to show us who we are (images of God) and how we are to act (we should reflect God in all we "think, and say, and do"), and to make it possible for us to reflect God.

1. **How do we learn about Jesus?** (From our parents, from our teachers, from the priests, and so forth.)
2. **Where do we hear stories about Jesus?** (At home, at school, at church during Mass.)
3. **Who is Jesus?** (Jesus is God the Son.)
4. **Why did Jesus become man?** (To show us we are images of God, to show us how to act as images of God, and to make it possible for us to act more like Jesus.)
5. **How do we show people that we are images of God?** (We should reflect God in all we "think, and say, and do".)
6. Ask the children to share their favorite Bible stories.

Extending the Lesson

Art and Craft Projects

Materials Needed
    A. Clothespins, white paper, scissors, tape.
    B. Milk cartons (half-pint), string, straws, hole punch.
    C. Black construction paper, white paper, yarn.

    A. Scroll. Give each child four clothespins and a piece of paper, 5 inches by 9 inches. Slide two clothespins, one on each side, at one end of the paper. Fold the edge of the paper over the clothespins and tape to secure. Attach the other two clothespins to the other end of the paper in the same way. Write "Jesus is God the Son" on the paper. Roll both ends of the paper toward the center to form a scroll. Remind the children of the purpose of a scroll. Jesus read the Scriptures, holy writings about God, from a scroll.
    B. Milk-carton Well. Remove the peaked top from a half-pint milk carton for each child. Punch a hole in two opposite sides of the carton. Slide a straw through the holes. On a small piece of paper write "Jesus is God the Son". Punch a hole in the paper. Attach the paper with string to the middle of the straw. Place the paper inside the carton. Show the children that, when the straw is turned, the note comes out of the carton. Remind the children of the story about the woman at the well. The woman believed Jesus was God the Son because He told her. We believe Jesus is God the Son because He tells us in the Bible through the Church.
    C. Construction-paper Bible. Place a sheet of white paper on top of a piece of black construction paper. Fold both papers in half. Place glue on the back of the white paper to hold it in place inside the black cover. Wrap a piece of yarn around both papers at the fold. On one half of the white paper write "Jesus is God the Son", and on the other half have the children draw a picture of their favorite Bible story.

Action Rhyme

    Open the Bible, (*Hold hands like an open book.*)
    And read "God made the whole world." (*Make a big circle with hands.*)
    Open the Bible, (*Hold hands like an open book.*)
    And read "God made you and me." (*Point to self and then to others.*)
    Open the Bible, (*Hold hands like an open book.*)
    And read "Jesus is God the Son."
    Open the Bible, (*Hold hands like an open book.*)
    And read "Jesus loves everyone." (*Hug self.*)

Prayer

    Dear Jesus, we believe You are God the Son. Help us always to try to be the best images of God we can be. Amen.

Worksheets

The worksheets can be sent home to be completed or can be completed in the classroom and then sent home. In either case, the worksheets should be used as take-home material because they furnish the basis for parent–child faith discussion.

Pre-school A. Worksheet 23 relates to the lesson theme and can be distributed to the children after the Application portion of the Lesson Presentation section to reinforce the concept. Worksheet 24 may be used after the Suggested Story to aid the children's retention of the story.

Pre-school B. Worksheet 75 can be used after the Suggested Story to aid the children's retention of the story. Worksheet 76 relates to the lesson theme and can be distributed to the children after the Application portion of the Lesson Presentation section to reinforce the concept.

Kindergarten. Worksheets 36 and 37 can each be used after its related Suggested Story to aid the children's retention of the story. Worksheet 38 can be distributed after the Living the Lesson section to help the children relate the theme to their daily lives.

Jesus Reads the Scriptures

One day Jesus went back to the town of Nazareth. He had lived there with Mary and Joseph when He was growing up. Jesus wanted the people of that town to know and love God.

Jesus went to the temple in Nazareth to pray. Someone asked Jesus to read the Scriptures from a scroll. Jesus chose to read a story telling about the person God was going to send to help the people. When Jesus finished reading, He began to talk to the people.

"What I have just read has already come true", Jesus said. "I am the Person sent from God." Jesus is God the Son.

"But you are Joseph's son", one man said.

"You are a carpenter", said another man.

The people became angry with Jesus. They would not believe Jesus.

"You want me to prove I am sent by God by doing miracles", Jesus said. "But I will not. I am the One the Scriptures tell about."

The people would not listen. They would not believe Jesus.

Jesus left Nazareth, but He did not stop teaching the people. He wanted everyone to know and believe in Him. He wanted to teach everyone how to act as images of God.

1. **Why did Jesus go to the temple?** (To pray.)
2. **What did the people ask Him to read?** (The Scriptures from a scroll.)
3. **Who did Jesus tell the people He was?** (The One sent by God to help the people.)
4. **Did the people believe Him?** (No.)
5. **Do we believe Jesus?** (Yes.)
6. **Who do we believe Jesus is?** (Jesus is God the Son.)

The Woman at the Well

Jesus went all over the country teaching the people about God. His friends, the Apostles, went with Him. One day, Jesus and His friends were walking along a hot, dusty road. After a long time, they stopped at a well to rest.

A woman came to the well to fill her pitcher with water. Jesus was very hot and thirsty.

"Give me a drink of water, please", He said to the woman.

The woman was very surprised. "Why are you talking to me? I do not know who you are", she said.

"If you knew Who I am, you would have asked me for something", Jesus told her. "I have something for you much better than a drink of water."

The woman stopped what she was doing and began to listen to Jesus. They talked for a long time. Jesus told the woman many things that He knew about her. All the time Jesus was talking, the woman may have been thinking, "I wonder if He is the One sent by God." Then the woman said to Jesus, "I know that God promised to send Someone Who would show us how to live."

Jesus must have looked at the woman very kindly as He said, "I am that Person. I was sent by God."

The woman had found something much better than water. She had found Jesus, God the Son.

Review Questions

1. **What did Jesus ask the woman to give Him?** (A drink of water.)
2. **Why was the woman surprised?** (Because she did not know Who Jesus was.)
3. **Who did the woman think Jesus was?** (The Person sent by God to show us how to live.)
4. **Who do we believe Jesus is?** (God the Son.)

Lesson 12   Miracles of Jesus

Workbook Pages

Pre-school A. 25–26
Pre-school B. 77–78
Kindergarten 39–41

Lesson Focus

In the Old Testament God told us about Himself, but in the New Testament God showed us Himself in Jesus. Jesus said, "Whoever has seen me has seen the Father" (John 14:9).

It is important in this lesson to establish the divinity of Jesus for the children. Jesus is God the Son. As God, He can do anything. The miracles that Jesus performed were not done by magic tricks. With magic tricks, something only seems to be happening. With miracles, something really does happen. For example, Jesus really did heal the sick, change water into wine, and multiply loaves and fishes. He could perform miracles because He is God.

The vocabulary word **miracle** can be defined for the children as something done to show the power of God and to help people believe in and follow Jesus. Miracles surprised and helped people. Jesus' miracles were *not magic*. Jesus is God the Son, and as God He can do anything.

Concepts of Faith

Who is Jesus?
   Jesus is God the Son.

Lesson Presentation

Application

The difference between magic and miracles will be stressed in this lesson. Magic should be explained to the children as a trick. Performing a simple magic trick and showing the children how it is done is an excellent way of demonstrating the trickery involved in magic. (The magic trick may be something as simple as hiding someone behind a door and then saying "open door". Have the person open the door without being seen by the children. Then bring out the hidden person so the children can see it was a trick. Or simple tricks can be found in books on magic or purchased at toy stores.)

Before disclosing the way the trick was done, ask the children if what you have just done is a miracle. Of course not! It was magic, because it was a trick.

Explain the special power of Jesus. He can do miracles because He is God. He did not need tricks to help the blind man see or the crippled people walk, or to turn water into wine. We can do tricks, but we cannot do miracles as Jesus did.

Sometimes the children may be confused, thinking that doctors work miracles as Jesus did. But Jesus did not need magic, medicine, or doctors to make people better. Ask the children if a doctor could fix someone's broken leg just by touching it. No, the doctor would give the person medicine to help the leg get better, but it would take a long time. Jesus is God the Son, and as God He can do anything. He could heal people just by touching them.

Discussion Questions

1. **Why could Jesus perform miracles?** (Because He is God the Son.)
2. **When we do a trick, is it magic or is it a miracle?** (We can do magic tricks, but we cannot do miracles.)
3. **Did Jesus need magic to do miracles?** (No.)

Suggested Stories

A. "Jesus' First Miracle" (based on John 2:1–11)
B. "A Miracle for Many" (based on John 6:1–15)

Living the Lesson

Jesus performed many miracles to help people. The miracles He worked helped people believe in what He said. As images of God, we can help others believe in and follow Jesus.

1. **When we see a magician on TV make a rabbit come out of a hat, or make someone disappear, is that a miracle?** (No, it is magic. It is a trick.)
2. **How did Jesus help the people who were sick?** (He cured them.)
3. **How do we help people who are sick?** (We take them to a doctor and give them medicine.) **Is that a miracle?** (No.)
4. **Where do we read about the miracles of Jesus?** (In the Bible.)

Extending the Lesson

Art and Craft Projects

Materials Needed
A. Water-jug pattern, construction paper, scissors, stapler.
B. Construction paper, yarn, fish pattern, scissors, tape.
C. Construction paper, crayons, scissors, rabbit-in-the-hat pattern, brads.

A. Water Jug. Using the pattern provided, cut one water jug for each child. Cut an opening as indicated. Using the same color paper as the water jug, cut two strips of colored paper, 3 inches by 1 inch. Staple these on either side of the opening as indicated. Cut one strip of white paper 2$\frac{1}{2}$ inches by 8 inches. Have the children color half the strip red. This strip will be the water and wine in the jug. Slide the "water and wine" strip through the slots made by the strips fastened on either side of the opening. Make sure the white

Use this pattern from the special pattern packet.

A.

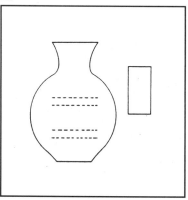

Use these patterns from the special pattern packet.

B.

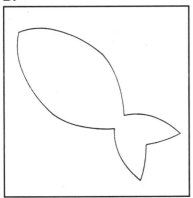

C.

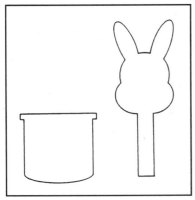

and red parts are visible through the opening. Write on the water jug "Jesus changes water into wine." Tell the children when the white is showing it will remind them of the water and when the red is showing it will remind them of the wine. Only Jesus can really change water into wine.

B. Fish Mobile. Using the pattern provided, cut from construction paper one large fish for each child. Cut several smaller fish from different colors of construction paper. If the children choose, they may decorate the fish. Hang the small fish from the large fish, using yarn. Write the words "Jesus can do miracles" on the large fish. Remind the children of the story about Jesus and the loaves and fishes. Tell them only Jesus can perform miracles. If we ran out of food, we would need to go to a grocery store or borrow from a friend. Jesus can do miracles because He is God the Son.

C. Magic Trick Picture. Cut a rabbit and a top hat for each child from the pattern provided. Have the children draw a face on the rabbit. Turn the top hat over and attach the rabbit with a brad. The brad should go through the hat near the brim and through the middle of the long strip below the rabbit. Show the children how the rabbit can be moved so it looks as if it is coming out of the hat. Tell the children that this is a trick. Only Jesus can do miracles. Write on the hat "Magic is a trick. Jesus does miracles."

Action Rhyme

Jesus worked some miracles
To help the people believe. (*Nod head "yes".*)
He changed water into wine, (*Pretend to pour water.*)
He made the blind man see. (*Cover eyes with hands, then remove hands.*)
He cured the little girl, (*Hug self.*)
And took her pain away. (*Open arms wide.*)
Jesus can do this and more,
For He is God the Son, you see. (*Nod head "yes".*)

Prayer

Dear Jesus, I know and believe that You are God the Son. Amen.

Worksheets

The worksheets can be sent home to be completed or can be completed in the classroom and then sent home. In either case, the worksheets should be used as take-home material because they furnish the basis for parent–child faith discussion.

Pre-school A. Worksheet 25 relates to the lesson theme and can be distributed to the children after the Application portion of the Lesson Presentation section to reinforce the concept or after the Living the Lesson section to help the children relate the theme to their daily lives. Worksheet 26 may be used after the Suggested Story to aid the children's retention of the story.

Pre-school B. Worksheet 77 relates to the lesson theme and can be distributed to the children after the Application portion of the Lesson Presentation section to reinforce the concept or after the Living the Lesson section to help the children relate the theme to their daily lives. Worksheet 78 can be used after its related Suggested Story to aid the children's retention of the story.

Kindergarten. Worksheets 39 and 40 can each be used after its related Suggested Story to aid the children's retention of the story. Worksheet 41 relates to the lesson theme and can be distributed to the children after the Application portion of the Lesson Presentation section to reinforce the concept or after the Living the Lesson section to help the children relate the theme to their daily lives.

Jesus' First Miracle

Two of Jesus' friends were getting married. They had invited Jesus, His special friends the Apostles, and Mary, His Mother, to the wedding. It was a big party with lots of people. Soon the groom, the man who got married, saw that the wine was almost gone. There was not enough left for the guests to drink with dinner. The groom felt very sad and did not know what to do. All the stores were closed, and he could not buy any more.

Mary, Jesus' Mother, saw the problem and wanted to help the groom so he would not be embarrassed.

She told Jesus, "Son, they have run out of wine."

It was not quite time for Jesus to start telling everyone about Himself, but He decided to help out His friend the groom. Besides, His Mother asked Him for this favor, and people like to do nice things for their mothers.

Jesus asked the waiters to fill six large pitchers with water. Then Jesus turned the water in the pitchers into wine. The groom was very surprised and happy. The wine Jesus made was much better than the wine that had run out.

This was the first miracle that Jesus worked. Only God can work a miracle. Jesus' special friends the Apostles were surprised at what happened, and they believed that Jesus was God the Son.

Review Questions

1. **What kind of party was Jesus invited to?** (A wedding.)
2. **What did the groom run out of?** (Wine.)
3. **Who asked Jesus to help the groom?** (Mary, Jesus' Mother.)
4. **Was changing the water to wine a magic trick?** (No.) **What was this called?** (A miracle.)
5. **Why can Jesus work miracles?** (Because He is God the Son.)

A Miracle for Many

One day a big crowd of people came to hear Jesus teach. Some of the people had traveled a very long way just to be near Him. They were so glad to be with Jesus, they did not even go home for lunch. It was getting late, and soon it would be supper time. They had listened to Jesus for hours and hours. Jesus knew the people must be hungry and tired after such a long day.

"We must fed these people", Jesus said to the Apostles.

The Apostles looked at the crowd. They could not even count all the people.

"We do not have enough money to buy food for all these people", they said. "Maybe we should send them home."

Just then, a little boy came to Jesus. He had heard Jesus talking to His helpers.

"I have five loaves of bread and two fish in my basket", he said. "I want you to have it."

Jesus took the basket from the boy. Then, as Jesus blessed the food, something wonderful happened. Instead of just five loaves and two fish, there was enough food to feed everyone!

The people could hardly believe their eyes. Jesus had worked a miracle.

Jesus did not use magic. Magic is a trick. Jesus did not use tricks. He worked miracles. Jesus is God the Son and, because He is God the Son, He can do anything.

Review Questions

1. **Why did all the people come to see Jesus?** (To hear Him teach and to be near Him.)
2. **Why did the Apostles want to send the people home?** (They did not have enough money to buy food for all the people.)
3. **What did the little boy give to Jesus?** (Five loaves of bread and two fish.)
4. **What did Jesus do with the bread and the fish?** (Blessed them.) **Then what happened?** (There was enough food for everyone.)
5. **Was this a trick?** (No.) **What was it?** (A miracle.)
6. **Why can Jesus work miracles?** (Because He is God the Son.)

Lesson 13 Jesus Says, "Come Follow Me"

Workbook Pages

Pre-school A. 27–28

Pre-school B. 79–80

Kindergarten 42–44

Lesson Focus

Jesus extended the invitation to follow Him repeatedly throughout His life on earth. He extended the invitation to follow Him (to do as He did) to the Apostles. They answered Jesus' call and chose to follow Him and to lead others to Him.

Apostles, the vocabulary word, can be explained to the children as special friends of Jesus who answered His call and chose to follow Him and teach others about Him.

Concepts of Faith

Who were the Apostles?

The Apostles were special friends of Jesus who answered His call and chose to follow Him and teach others about Him.

Lesson Presentation

Application

Show the children a picture of Jesus and the Apostles. Children often think of the Apostles as "superheroes" or extraordinary men. Explain to the children that the twelve Apostles who answered Jesus' call were not the richest, strongest, or wisest men. Nor did they have the most friends or the nicest clothes.

They answered Jesus' call because they believed in Him and loved Him. The Apostles wanted to teach others what Jesus had taught them.

As you show the children the picture of Jesus and the Apostles, tell them something about each Apostle.

1. **Andrew.** Andrew was a fisherman. John the Baptist had taught Andrew about God. Andrew was at the river when Jesus was baptized. Jesus invited Andrew to follow Him. Andrew was the first Apostle.

2. **Peter.** Peter and Andrew were brothers. Andrew brought Peter to Jesus. Peter chose to follow Jesus too. Later, Peter served as the first Pope of the Church.

3. **John.** John was the youngest Apostle. Before Jesus died, He asked John to take care of His Mother, Mary. John wrote down the stories about Jesus so all people would know about Him. We call these stories Gospels. We can read the Gospel of John in the Bible.

4. **James.** Jesus asked two men named James to be Apostles. The first James was called James the Greater, because he was older than the other James. Jesus told James the Greater that He would make him a "fisher of men".

5. **James the Less.** The second James was called James the Less, because he was younger. We remember James because he told the people to show their love for God in their prayers.

6. **Matthew.** Some people did not like Matthew, because he was a tax collector. He collected money from the people and gave it to the king. When Jesus asked Matthew to follow Him, Matthew left his money and his work to be with Jesus. Matthew wrote stories about Jesus' life on earth. We call these stories about Jesus' life on earth Gospels. We can read the Gospel of Matthew in the Bible.

7. **Philip.** John the Baptist told Philip about Jesus. When Philip heard about Jesus, he chose to follow Him. Then Philip brought his friend Bartholomew to Jesus.

8. **Bartholomew.** At first, Bartholomew did not believe Jesus was God the Son. Jesus called Bartholomew by name and told Bartholomew where he had come from and what he had been doing. Then Bartholomew believed in Jesus and chose to follow Him.

9. **Thomas.** Thomas would not believe that Jesus had risen from the dead. He wanted to see and touch Jesus to be sure. Then Jesus appeared to Thomas. When Thomas saw Jesus, he believed that Jesus had risen from the dead.

10. **Simon.** Simon was Jesus' cousin. Simon told Jesus he would protect Him from those people who wanted to harm Jesus. Some people wanted Simon to turn away from Jesus, but Simon would not listen. He wanted all people to love Jesus.

11. **Jude Thaddeus.** Jude was also a cousin of Jesus. He wrote letters to teach the people that God is most important. He followed Jesus by teaching the people about God's love.

12. **Matthias.** Jesus had died, had risen from the dead, and had gone to heaven. One of the Apostles who followed Jesus had died, too. The Apostles needed to choose someone to be the twelfth Apostle. They chose Matthias. Matthias had spent time listening to Jesus teach. Matthias believed in Jesus and wanted to teach others about Him.

Remind the children that these men answered Jesus' call to follow Him. Jesus wanted them to show and teach others how to live as images of God. Jesus invites all of us to follow Him and act as images of God.

Discussion Questions

1. **How many Apostles were there?** (Twelve.)
2. **Why did the Apostles follow Jesus?** (Because they believed in Him, loved Him, and wanted to teach others about Him.)
3. **Which of the Apostles wrote stories about Jesus?** (Matthew and John.)
4. **What do we call these stories?** (Gospels.)
5. **Where do we find these stories?** (In the Bible.)

Suggested Stories

A. "Fishers of Men" (based on Luke 5:1–11)
B. "Come Follow Me" (based on Matthew 4:18–22)

Living the Lesson

Jesus asks all people to follow Him. We follow Jesus by being the best image of God that we can be.

1. **Whom should we follow?** (Jesus.)
2. **Are we ever too young to follow Jesus?** (No.)
3. **How do we show we are followers of Jesus?** (By believing what the Church teaches, following the Ten Commandments, and acting as images of God.)

Extending the Lesson

Art and Craft Projects

Materials Needed

A. Sandpaper (fine grade), brown construction paper, glue, scissors.

B. Construction paper in pink, white, brown, black, red, and yellow; scissors; yarn; netting.

C. Poster board, sandal pattern, shoelaces or yarn, hole punch.

A. Footsteps Picture. Each child will need a piece of sandpaper (approximately 5 by 7 inches) and small footprints cut from construction paper. Remind the children that some of the Apostles were fishermen. The Apostles left their boats and nets by the sea and followed Jesus. Give the children five or more pairs of little footprints. Have them glue the footprints on the sandpaper. Label the picture "The Apostles followed Jesus".

B. Fishers-of-Men Nets. Each child will need a paper doll, 3 inches tall, cut from pink, white, brown, black, red, and yellow construction paper. Give each child a 6- by 6-inch piece of netting. Tell the children to place the six paper dolls in the center of the netting and tie it with yarn to form a bag. Attach a note to the bag reading "I will make you fishers of men." Remind the children of the story about the calling of the Apostles. Jesus calls all of us to follow Him. By reflecting God in all we "think, and say, and do", we can be fishers of men too. We can teach others about Jesus.

C. Sandals. Using the pattern provided, cut two sandals from poster board for each child. Using a hole punch, make four holes in each sandal as indicated on the pattern. Lace the yarn or shoelace through the holes, starting at hole A and finishing with hole D. These sandals remind us of the kind of shoes Jesus and the Apostles wore. We want to follow Jesus' example. We want to act as images of God in all we "think, and say, and do".

Use this pattern from the special pattern packet.

C.

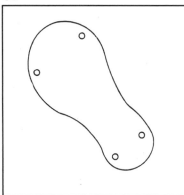

Action Rhyme

> Come follow Jesus, (*With your hand, make a coming motion.*)
> In all you think, and say, and do. (*Point to head, mouth, and hands.*)
> Come follow Jesus, (*With your hand, make a coming motion.*)
> Show your love is true. (*Place hands on heart.*)

Prayer

> Heavenly Father, help me follow the example of Your Son, Jesus. Amen.

Worksheets

The worksheets can be sent home to be completed or can be completed in the classroom and then sent home. In either case, the worksheets should be used as take-home material because they furnish the basis for parent–child faith discussion.

Pre-school A. Worksheets 27 and 28 can be used after the Suggested Story to aid the children's retention of the story.

Pre-school B. Worksheet 79 can be used after the Suggested Story to aid the children's retention of the story. Worksheet 80 can be distributed after the Living the Lesson section to help the children relate the theme to their daily lives.

Kindergarten. Worksheets 42–44 can each be used after its related Suggested Story to aid the children's retention of the story.

Fishers of Men

One day Jesus was talking to a large crowd of people by the sea. The crowd came closer, and closer, and closer to Jesus. They came so close they almost pushed Jesus into the water! Jesus saw two boats by the shore. He got into the boat that Peter owned. Jesus asked Peter to take Him a little way out into the water so He could talk to the people better.

When Jesus finished talking to the people, He asked Peter to take the boat out to the deeper water.

"Throw in your nets", He told Peter. "And you will catch some fish."

"I am very tired from fishing all night", Peter said. "And I did not catch anything. But, if You say so, I will try again."

Peter threw the nets into the deep water and waited. Then Peter tried to lift the nets back into the boat, but he could not lift them. The nets were so full of fish he could not budge them an inch! Peter called to his friends James and John to bring their boats and come help him.

Peter could not believe what had happened. He knelt down in front of Jesus and thanked Him.

Jesus told Peter, "From now on you will be catching men."

Peter believed in Jesus and what He taught. Peter helped teach many other people about Jesus.

Review Questions

1. **Why did Jesus get into the boat?** (Because the crowd was coming so close they almost pushed Jesus into the water.)
2. **Whose boat did Jesus get into?** (Peter's boat.)
3. **What did Jesus tell Peter to do with the nets?** (Lower the nets into deep water and try to catch fish.)
4. **Did Peter think he was going to catch any fish?** (No.)
5. **What happened?** (Peter caught so many fish he could not pull in the net.)
6. **What did Jesus say that Peter would catch from now on?** (Men.)

Come Follow Me

Jesus wanted to teach everyone about God, but there were so many people He could not do it by Himself. Jesus chose twelve men to help Him. We call these men the twelve Apostles.

One day Jesus went for a walk by the Sea of Galilee. Groups of fishermen were sitting near the shore. Some of the men were Jesus' friends.

"Andrew! Peter!" called Jesus as He waved at one boat. Andrew and Peter heard Jesus and rowed to shore.

"Come follow Me", Jesus said. "You are good fishermen, but I will make you fishers of men."

Andrew and Simon were not sure what Jesus meant, but they loved Jesus and wanted to follow Him. Just then, Jesus saw James and John. They were busy mending their nets.

"James! John!" Jesus called. "Come follow Me."

James and John put down their nets and followed Jesus. Jesus wanted these men to learn from Him so they could help Him teach others.

Jesus invites all people to follow Him. We follow Jesus by believing what the Church teaches, following the Ten Commandments, and by loving others. We follow Jesus by trying to be the best images of God we can be.

Review Questions

1. **What did Andrew, Peter, James, and John do before they became followers of Jesus?** (They were fishermen.)
2. **What did Jesus say to His friends.** (Come follow Me.)
3. **What did Jesus say they would become?** (Fishers of men.)

Lesson 13K   Jesus, Our Example

Workbook Pages
Kindergarten 45–46

Lesson Focus

This lesson is an extension for kindergarten of Lesson 13, "Jesus Says, 'Come Follow Me' ". The material is designed for one class period.

Jesus is our perfect example. He shows us God and, therefore, how we should live as images of God. Everything we do, except sin, He did. He was angry. He was overjoyed. He worked. He played. He suffered. He loved. He had friends. Everything we experience, except sin, He experienced. These human emotions and activities become worthy of God because God experienced them. In Christ, every human activity, except sin, is raised to the level of divine.

The vocabulary word is **example**. Tell the children an example shows us how something is done. Jesus is our example. He taught us how to be the best images of God we can be. When we follow Jesus' example, we reflect God in all we "think, and say, and do".

Concepts of Faith

Who is our perfect example?
Jesus is our perfect example.

How do we follow Jesus' example?
We follow Jesus' example by doing what Jesus did.

Lesson Presentation

Application

This presentation is an introduction to the corporal works of mercy. We introduce them as the good works we can do to follow Jesus' example. Describe them as follows:

1. Feed the hungry; give drink to the thirsty. When we give food to the poor and money to the missions, we are following Jesus' example.

2. Clothe the naked. Sometimes we give the clothes that we have outgrown to other people who need clothes. When we share in this way, we are doing good works.

3. Shelter and welcome the homeless. We can do this good work by being friendly to children who are new in our school and in our neighborhood.

4. Visit and comfort the sick and imprisoned. We can visit friends and neighbors when they are sick. We can make cards or bring flowers to someone who does not feel well.

5. Bury the dead. We can pray for those who have died and ask God to welcome them to His loving care.

When we follow Jesus' example, we become the best images of God we can be.

Living the Lesson

1. If there is an absent child, have the class make a card for that child.

2. If there is a nursing home or hospital nearby, have the children make cards or tray favors for the patients.

3. The children could visit a nearby nursing home and sing for the residents.

Extending the Lesson

Action Rhyme

I want God to hear, (*Hand points to ear.*)
I want God to see, (*Point to eyes.*)
That I'm the best image of God I can be. (*Point to self.*)
I give Him my prayers, (*Fold hands.*)
I give Him my love, (*Hug self.*)
I know He watches me from above.

Prayer

Dear God, help me follow Jesus' example so I can reflect You in all I "think, and say, and do". Amen.

Worksheets

The worksheets can be sent home to be completed or can be completed in the classroom and then sent home. In either case, the worksheets should be used as take-home material because they furnish the basis for parent–child faith discussion.

Kindergarten. Worksheet 45 can be distributed after the vocabulary word has been introduced. Worksheet 46 can be distributed after the Living the Lesson section to help the children relate the theme to their daily lives.

Lesson 14 Faith and Trust

Workbook Pages
Pre-school A. 29–30
Pre-school B. 81–82
Kindergarten 47–49

Lesson Focus

Faith is believing in God. Even though we cannot see or touch God, we believe that there are three Persons—Father, Son, and Holy Spirit—in one God.

Faith without expression dies. We as teachers, by our example, teach the children the fundamentals of the Faith and the importance of faith in our lives. When we follow the teaching of the Church, go to Mass, receive the sacraments, and lead good lives, we are living our faith.

Faith, the vocabulary word, can be explained as believing in God. We believe in God even though we cannot see Him.

Concepts of Faith

What is faith?

Faith is believing in God, even though we cannot see Him.

Lesson Presentation

Application

Show the children a deflated balloon. Ask them what is inside the balloon. (*Nothing.*) Now blow up the balloon and hold the end secure. Ask the children what is in the balloon now. (*Air.*) Tell the children you are going to dump the air out of the balloon all over them. Tell them to catch the air and hold it in their hands. Can they see the air? (*No.*) Can they catch it? (*No.*) Stress that we know there is air in the balloon even though we cannot see it.

Explain that the air in the balloon helps us understand faith. We cannot see God or touch Him, but we know He is with us. Even though God does not hug us or hold our hand, we know He loves us, because He made us in His image and He died on the Cross for us. Even when we are busy thinking about other things, God is never too busy for us. We have faith in God; we believe in Him.

Discussion Questions

1. **What is faith?** (Faith is believing in God, even though we cannot see Him.)
2. **Can we see or touch God?** (No, but we believe He is with us.)
3. **Does God love us?** (Yes, He made us in His image, and He died on the Cross for us.)
4. **Is God ever too busy to listen to our prayers?** (No.)

Suggested Stories

A. "Jesus Calms the Storm" (based on Luke 8:22–25)
B. "Noah's Ark" (based on Genesis 6:14–22, 8:6–12, 9:8–17)

Living the Lesson

God made us to do good things. When we live good lives, we are showing our faith and saying "Yes" to God. Jesus, God the Son, teaches us what are truly good actions. By following Jesus' example and the teachings of His Church, we practice our faith and show God our love.

1. **Who teaches us to have faith in God?** (Parents, teachers, priests, grandparents, and so forth.)
2. **How do we show we have faith in God?** (By going to church, by learning about God, by always trying to act as images of God, and so forth.)
3. **Should we want to learn about God?** (Yes, so our faith will grow.)

Extending the Lesson

Art and Craft Projects

Materials Needed

   A. Pattern for boat and wave, hole punch, brads, construction paper.

   B. Ark pattern, construction paper, animal cookies, glue.

   C. Construction paper, magazines, brad, glue.

   A. Boat and Wave Picture. Using the pattern provided, cut a boat and wave from construction paper for each child. Punch a hole toward the bottom of the boat and the middle of the wave. Take care to center the wave on the boat. Secure the two pieces with a brad. Write "Jesus calmed the storm" on the wave. Remind the children of the story of Jesus calming the storm. Explain how Jesus' friends the Apostles put their trust in Jesus. They believed that Jesus would take care of them. Show the children how the boat is able to rock on the wave. (Move the boat back and forth, keeping the wave still.) Have the children act out the story.

   B. Noah's Ark. Using the ark pattern, cut one ark for each child from construction paper. Glue the ark on a larger piece of construction paper. Give the children several animal crackers. Have the children glue the crackers around and on the ark. (You may want to provide the children with some crackers to eat.) Remind the children of Noah's faith and trust in God. Noah believed what God told him. Noah believed God would take care of him and his family. He believed God would be with him always. Noah practiced his faith by doing all that God wanted and living a good life.

   C. Picture Wheel. Cut two circles of the same size from construction paper. Draw lines dividing one of the circles into four equal sections. This will be the bottom of the picture wheel. Cut one section from the other circle. This will be the top of the wheel. Draw four pictures or cut four pictures from a magazine showing places where God is with us. (At home, at school, at play, at church, while we are eating, while we are sleeping, in the hospital, and so on.) Place one picture in each section of the bottom wheel. Punch a hole

Use these patterns from the special pattern packet.

A.

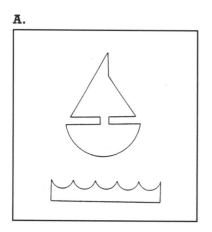

B.

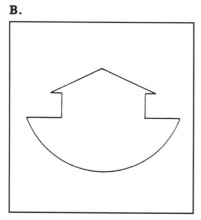

in the center of both circles. Insert a brad through both circles. As the bottom circle is turned, a new picture will appear in the opening of the top circle. Write "God is with me at" on the top circle. Allow the children time to practice with their picture wheels while you explain to them that God is always with us.

Action Rhyme

I have a very special friend, (*Point to self.*)
That no one here can see, (*Cover eyes.*)
You cannot even touch His hand,
But I know He's here with me. (*Point to heart.*)
My special friend is Jesus. (*Point to heaven.*)
I believe He hears my prayers. (*Fold hands.*)
I believe He loves me, oh so much. (*Hug self.*)
He's here and everywhere. (*Open arms wide.*)

Prayer

Dear God, I believe You are always with me. I will show my faith in all I "think, and say, and do". Amen.

Worksheets

The worksheets can be sent home to be completed or can be completed in the classroom and then sent home. In either case, the worksheets should be used as take-home material because they furnish the basis for parent–child faith discussion.

Pre-school A. Worksheet 29 can be used after the Suggested Story to aid the children's retention of the story. Worksheet 30 relates to the lesson theme and can be distributed to the children after the Application portion of the Lesson Presentation section to reinforce the concept.

Pre-school B. Worksheets 81 and 82 can be used after their related Suggested Story to aid the children's retention of the story.

Kindergarten. Worksheets 47 and 49 can each be used after its related Suggested Story to aid the children's retention of the story. Worksheet 48 can be distributed after the Living the Lesson section to help the children relate the theme to their daily lives.

Jesus Calms the Storm

Jesus sometimes went with His friends the Apostles in their fishing boat. One day Jesus asked His friends to take Him across the lake. The lake was very deep and wide, but they did what Jesus asked.

Jesus was very tired and took a nap in the back of the boat. While Jesus was sleeping, the sky suddenly got very dark. It began to rain very hard, and there were great gusts of wind. The waves got bigger and bigger. Soon the water started to come into the boat. Jesus' friends were very afraid!

"Wake up, Jesus!" they cried. "It's storming, and we're all going to drown!"

Jesus stood up and smiled at His friends. He looked across the water. Jesus commanded the wind and the water to be still. Right away, the wind stopped, and the water calmed down. The storm stopped.

All the Apostles wondered Who Jesus was that the wind and the water obeyed Him.

We know that Jesus is God the Son. We believe in God. We have faith. We believe that God hears all our prayers. We believe that God is with us always—when we are afraid, or lonely, happy, or sad.

Review Questions

1. **What did Jesus ask His friends to do?** (Take Him across the lake.)
2. **What did Jesus do when He was in the boat?** (He took a nap.)
3. **What happened when Jesus was sleeping?** (A storm came up.)
4. **How did Jesus' friends feel?** (They were afraid.)
5. **What did Jesus do?** (Jesus stopped the storm.)
6. **Why could Jesus do this?** (Because He is God the Son.)
7. **When is God with us?** (God is with us always.)

Noah's Ark

Noah was a kind and good man. He loved God and believed in Him. He knew God would take care of him always. God was pleased with Noah because Noah tried to do what was right.

God told Noah to build a big boat called an ark. "It must be big enough for you, your family, and two of every kind of animal and creature", God said. "Soon a flood will cover the earth, but I will keep you safe in the ark."

Building the big boat was not easy, but Noah obeyed God. Noah and his family worked very hard together. Sometimes people would stop and laugh at them. "You do not need a boat on dry land", the people said. "You should forget about this silly boat and come have fun with us."

But Noah and his family did not stop working. "This is what God wants us to do", they said. "God knows what is best for us. We believe in God."

When the boat was finished and the shelves were filled with food, Noah led two of every kind of animal and creature inside.

Then Noah and his family climbed inside. Soon it began to rain. It rained for forty days and forty nights. The water rose higher and higher until the highest mountain was covered with water. God kept Noah and his family and all the animals safe from the flood in the big boat that He had told Noah to build.

At last the rain stopped. Noah opened a window of the boat and sent out a dove. When the dove returned, it was carrying a branch from an olive tree. Noah knew that soon all the water would be gone. God sent a great wind to dry up all the water. Then God told Noah to come out. The door of the boat opened, and all the animals were set free. Noah and his family thanked God for keeping them safe. Then a beautiful rainbow filled the sky. "This rainbow is a sign of My love for you. I will never again send a flood to cover the whole earth", God said. "The rainbow is a reminder of this promise."

We believe in God and obey Him, as Noah did. Even though we cannot see or touch God, we know He is with us wherever we go. God hears our prayers and takes care of us. He keeps us safe in His love. When we live our faith, we act as images of God.

Review Questions

1. **What did God tell Noah to do?** (Build a big boat.) **What was the boat called?** (An ark.)
2. **Why did Noah do as God said?** (Because Noah loved God and believed in Him.)
3. **Who went on the ark?** (Noah, his family, and two of every kind of animal.)
4. **What was the rainbow a sign of?** (God's love and a reminder that God would never send a flood to cover the whole earth again.)
5. **What did Noah and his family do when they left the boat?** (They thanked God for keeping them safe.)

Lesson 14K The Rosary

Workbook Page
Kindergarten 50

Lesson Focus

This lesson is an extension for kindergarten of Lesson 14, "Faith and Trust". The material is designed for one class period. This extension is an introduction to the Rosary.

In praying the Rosary, we pray the Joyful, the Sorrowful, and the Glorious Mysteries. We reflect on special events in Jesus' life. We ask Mary to pray for us and lead us to her Son.

The vocabulary word is **Rosary**. Explain to the children that the Rosary is made up of a certain number of different prayers, the "Hail Mary", the "Our Father", and the "Glory Be". When we pray the Rosary, we think about special events in Jesus' life. The rosary beads help us count the number of prayers that we have said. When we pray the Rosary, we ask Mary to ask Jesus to keep us in His loving care.

Concepts of Faith

What does the Rosary help us remember?
The Rosary helps us remember special events in Jesus' life.

Lesson Presentation

Application

Show the children a rosary. Point out the cross. The cross helps us remember that Jesus loved us so much He died on the Cross for us. Tell the children that we begin the Rosary by holding the cross and saying a prayer called the "Apostles' Creed". In this prayer we say we believe in God the Father, God the Son, and God the Holy Spirit. We also say we believe that Jesus died for us and rose from the dead. We say we believe in all that Jesus taught us.

Next show the children the different beads. Tell the children that on the larger beads, the beads that are all alone, we say the "Our Father". On the beads that are all in a row, we say the "Hail Mary". Tell the children there is one more prayer that makes up the Rosary. It is the "Glory Be". We pray the "Glory Be" when we come to the space before each of the big "Our Father" beads. Explain to the children that we say one "Our Father", ten "Hail Marys", and one "Glory Be" five times to make up one Rosary.

Discussion Questions

1. **Where do we start when we pray the Rosary?** (On the cross.)
2. **What prayer do we pray on the bead that is all alone?** (The "Our Father".)
3. **What prayer do we pray on the beads that are all in a row?** (The "Hail Mary".)

4. **What prayer do we pray in the space before each "Our Father"?** (The "Glory Be".)
5. **What do we think about when we pray the Rosary?** (Jesus' life.)

Living the Lesson

Review the "Our Father" and its meaning from Lesson 10 and the "Glory Be" and its meaning from Lesson 1. The "Hail Mary" and its meaning are discussed in Lesson 21.

Lead the children in one decade of the Rosary. Tell the children that, even though they may not be able to say all the prayers of the Rosary, they can pray some of them. Remind them that the rosary beads are not a toy to be played with, but something special that Mary gave us to help us remember Jesus' life and how much He loves us.

Worksheet

The worksheet can be sent home to be completed or can be completed in the classroom and then sent home. In either case, the worksheet should be used as take-home material because it furnishes the basis for parent–child faith discussion.

Kindergarten. Worksheet 50 relates to the lesson theme and can be distributed to the children after the Application portion of the Lesson Presentation section to reinforce the concept or after the Living the Lesson section to help the children relate the theme to their daily lives.

Lesson 15   After Death There Is Life

Workbook Pages
Pre-school A. 31–32
Pre-school B. 83–84
Kindergarten 51–53

Lesson Focus

Jesus said, "I am the resurrection and the life: whoever believes in Me, though he should die, will come to life, and whoever is alive and believes in Me will never die" (John 11:25–26).

It is through following Jesus and living as He taught that we find eternal life in heaven. When we die, it is not the end of our lives; rather, it is the separation of our bodies and our souls. It is the end of our lives on earth and, we hope, the beginning of everlasting life with our Father in heaven. We remember Jesus' Resurrection, when He triumphed over death. Through His divine acts of love, the Cross and the Resurrection, He has made it possible for all people to share in everlasting life with God.

Our vocabulary word, **dying**, should be explained as a change from one kind of life to another. When someone dies, that person's life does not end; it changes. If we have lived as images of God, dying is the beginning of a new life with God.

Concepts of Faith

Is dying the end of our lives?
No, if we have lived as images of God then it is the beginning of new life with God in heaven.

Lesson Presentation

Application

Tell the children that when we die our lives do not end, they change. When people die, they begin new lives with God in heaven, if they have followed Jesus' example. We are still images of God even after we have died.

To illustrate this concept, you will need a clear bowl of ice (or snow) and a bowl of water. Show the children the bowl of ice. Ask what happens when the ice melts. Does it disappear? No, it changes. Show the children the bowl of water. Tell them that, when the ice melts, it changes to water. The ice is still in the bowl, but it has changed. Explain to the children that, when people die, they no longer live on earth. Their lives have changed. If they have acted as images of God, they have begun new life with God in heaven.

Discussion Questions

1. **When people die, is that the end of their lives?** (No, they begin new lives with God in heaven, if they have followed Jesus' example.)
2. **Who made it possible for us to share in the new life with God?** (Jesus.)
3. **How?** (By dying on the Cross for us and rising from the dead.)

Suggested Stories

A. "Lazarus" (based on John 11:17–44)
B. "Jesus and the Little Girl" (based on Mark 5:21–24, 35–43)

Living the Lesson

There may be some confusion in the children's minds in regard to death. Through exposure to television, they have seen a person "die" as one character and later reappear as another character. It is important that the children understand this is "just pretend". When people die, they do not come back to earth in other bodies. If they have acted as images of God, they begin a new life with God in heaven. We pray for all those who have died so they may receive new life with God in heaven.

1. Ask the children if they know someone who has died. **Did they feel sad when that person died?** It is all right to feel sad when people die, because we will miss them here on earth. We must remember that, if they have acted as images of God, they have started new lives with God in heaven. The people who die are not sick anymore but are happy with God in heaven.

2. **Do we still think about people after they have died?** (Yes, we remember them, and we pray for them.)

Extending the Lesson

Art and Craft Projects

Materials Needed
    A. Cotton balls, glue, construction paper, butterfly pattern, pipe cleaners, craft sticks, crayons.
    B. Styrofoam or clear plastic cups, seeds, soil.

    A. Cocoons and Butterflies. Give each child a craft stick and some cotton balls. Have the children glue cotton balls completely covering one side of the craft stick. This is a cocoon. Cut a butterfly (pattern provided) from construction paper for each child. Have the children decorate the butterfly any way they would like. Use a pipe cleaner as the butterfly's antennae. Curve the ends of the pipe cleaner and attach it to the head of the butterfly. Glue the cocoon and the butterfly side by side on a large piece of construction paper. Label the project "A butterfly is a sign of new life". Tell the children a butterfly is a sign of new life in the spring. It begins as a caterpillar and then changes into something wonderful—a butterfly. Tell the children that when people die it is not the end of their lives. Something wonderful happens—they begin new life with God in heaven.
    B. Planting Seeds. Give each child a styrofoam or clear plastic cup. Have the children fill the cups half or three-quarters full of soil. Give each child three or four seeds to plant. (Bean seeds work especially well, because they grow rapidly.) Explain to the children that in the springtime we see many things that remind us of new life.

Use this pattern from the special pattern packet.

A.

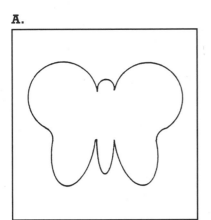

Trees are blooming, grass is turning green, and flowers are beginning to come through the ground. Their plants will help the children remember the new life they can share someday in heaven with God. We plant a seed (that looks dead) to grow new plants. When people die, their lives do not end. It is the beginning of new life with God in heaven.

Action Rhyme

God will give new life to me. (*Arms raised up.*)
Up in heaven I will be.
He will open His gates wide, (*Open arms wide.*)
I will gladly run inside. (*Run in place.*)
Yes, I will love Him, (*Nod head "yes".*)
Yes, I will love Him,
With God I want to be.

Prayer

Dear God, we thank You for the gift of new life. We want to be with You someday in heaven. Amen.

Worksheets

The worksheets can be sent home to be completed or can be completed in the classroom and then sent home. In either case, the worksheets should be used as take-home material because they furnish the basis for parent–child faith discussion.

Pre-school A. Worksheets 31 and 32 relate to the lesson theme and can be distributed to the children after the Application portion of the Lesson Presentation section to reinforce the concept or after the Living the Lesson section to help the children relate the theme to their daily lives.

Pre-school B. Worksheet 83 can be used after the Suggested Story to aid the children's retention of the story. Worksheet 84 relates to the lesson theme and can be distributed to the children after the Application portion of the Lesson Presentation section to reinforce the concept or after the Living the Lesson section to help the children relate the theme to their daily lives.

Kindergarten. Worksheets 51 to 53 relate to the lesson theme and can be distributed to the children after the Application portion of the Lesson Presentation section to reinforce the concept or after the Living the Lesson section to help the children relate the theme to their daily lives.

Lazarus

Jesus had many friends. Two sisters named Martha and Mary and their brother, Lazarus, were good friends of Jesus. When their brother, Lazarus, died, Mary and Martha were very sad. They sent for Jesus. As Jesus came near, Martha ran out to meet Him. Martha said, "Lord, if you had been here, my brother would never had died."

Jesus said, "Your brother will rise again. I am the resurrection and the life; whoever believes in Me will come to life."

Both Martha and Mary were very sad. They sat close to Jesus. After seeing their tears and the sadness of Lazarus' other friends, Jesus cried too.

Jesus went to the place where Lazarus was buried. He knelt down and prayed. Then Jesus called with a loud voice, "Lazarus, come out!" Then Lazarus came out! Many of the people then believed in Jesus.

When Jesus said "I am the resurrection and the life; whoever believes in Me will come to life", He meant that, if we believe in Him and follow His example, we will be with Him in heaven someday. All people die someday. That means that they do not live on earth anymore. We cannot see them. But they do live in heaven if they believed in Jesus and followed His example. We remember them, and we pray for them. We hope that someday we will all be together in heaven.

Review Questions

1. **What were the names of the two sisters in the story?** (Mary and Martha.)
2. **Why were Mary and Martha sad?** (Because their brother, Lazarus, had died.)
3. **Was Lazarus a friend of Jesus too?** (Yes.)
4. **Was Jesus sad?** (Yes, Jesus cried.)
5. **What did Jesus do for Lazarus?** (Prayed and brought him back to life.)
6. **How could Jesus do this?** (Because He is God the Son.)
7. **How do we remember those who have died?** (We pray for them.)

Jesus and the Little Girl

One day a man named Jairus asked Jesus to help him. Jairus' daughter was very sick and could die. No matter what Jairus did, his little girl did not get any better.

Jesus went home with Jairus. On the way, a neighbor of Jairus stopped them. "Do not bother Jesus", he said to Jairus. "You are too late. Your daughter is dead."

Jairus felt very sad when he heard this. But Jesus said, "Do not be sad, Jairus. Trust in me."

When they reached Jairus' house, they saw many people. The people were all very sad and were crying. "Why are you crying?" Jesus asked. "The little girl is not dead. She is only sleeping."

Then Jesus went into the little girl's room. She was lying still. Jesus took her hand and placed it in His. "Little girl, get up", Jesus said. Just as Jesus said this, the little girl opened her eyes and sat up! Jairus and his wife were very happy. They were so happy to see their little girl alive and well. Jesus had brought the little girl back to life. Jairus and his wife thanked Jesus, and from then on they believed in Him.

Review Questions

1. **Why did Jairus need Jesus' help?** (His little girl was very sick.)
2. **What news did Jairus' neighbor bring?** (The little girl had died.)
3. **What did Jesus do when He saw the little girl?** (Took her hand and brought her back to life.)
4. **Is dying the end of our lives?** (No, dying is the beginning of new life with God, if we have acted as images of God.)

God Should Come First in Our Lives

Workbook Pages
Pre-school A. 33–34
Pre-school B. 85–86
Kindergarten 54–55

Lesson Focus

We share God's life on earth, and we prepare ourselves for the joy of eternal life with God in heaven. Jesus taught us by His example that God is most important in our lives. Through our prayers, our sacrifices, and our acts of love, we are following Jesus' example.

It should be explained that sometimes we let material things become more important than God. Explain to the children that all we have comes from God and that God always knows what is best for us. Help the children understand that the things we have or who we are in the community are not really important. What should be important to us is how we live our lives as images of God. When we live our lives showing we are images of God in all we "think, and say, and do", then we show that God comes first for us.

The vocabulary word is **important**. Explain to the children that someone or something important means a lot to us.

Concepts of Faith

Who is most important in our lives?
God is most important in our lives.

How do we show that God is most important?
We show that God is most important by acting as an image of God in all we "think, and say, and do".

Lesson Presentation

Application

It is important that the children learn to realize that their Faith is more valuable than the material objects they possess or want. In today's society, peer pressure starts very early. Even very young children receive the message, through the media and their friends, that wearing the right clothes or being friends with the right people or owning the right items makes them important. In this lesson, comparisons are made between religious articles and other common items.

Stress the importance of the religious articles, because they help us learn about God. You will need a Bible, a comic book (or other story book), a rosary, a necklace, a picture of a large house, a picture of a church, a crucifix, and some small knickknack (such as a ceramic figure).

Show the children the Bible and the comic book. Ask them which is more important. The Bible is more important, because it helps us learn about God. Next, show the rosary and a necklace. (If the children are not familiar with a rosary, you may want to point out to the children the cross on the rosary and briefly explain that we keep track of prayers on the rosary beads.) Which is more important? The rosary is more important, because it is a prayer to Mary, the Mother of God. The rosary also helps us think about events in the life of Jesus. Because we say prayers on the rosary, we should treat it with care. It is not a toy to be played with. Show the children a picture of a house and a picture of a church. Which building, a fancy house or God's house, is more important? God's house is more important. We are on our best behavior when we go to God's house. Show the children the crucifix and the figurine. Which is more important? The crucifix helps us remember that Jesus loves us so much He died for us.

Explain to the children that things—toys, jewelry, houses, money, and so forth—are good and are for our use, but they are not the most important part of life. God should be number one in our lives. When we learn about God, pray to Him, worship Him, and act as images of God, we show that God is most important in our lives.

Discussion Questions

1. **Who should be most important in our lives?** (God.)
2. **How do we show that God is important in our lives?** (By learning about God, praying to Him, worshiping Him, and by acting as images of God.)
3. **Are money and other things we have more important than God?** (No.)
4. **How do we treat the Bible, a rosary, a crucifix, things we find in church, and other things that help us come to know about God?** (With care and respect.)
5. **Are they toys to be played with?** (No.)

Suggested Stories

A. "Jesus in the Desert" (based on Luke 4:1–13)
B. "The House on the Rock" (based on Matthew 7:24–29)

Living the Lesson

Help the children understand that all the material things we have are not as important as God. Neither is being the prettiest, nor the tallest, nor the fastest, nor the smartest, nor the richest. When we choose to live as images of God, we are showing that God is important to us. It may not always be easy to do what is right, but when we obey and think of others before ourselves, we are living as Jesus taught and showing that God is most important in our lives.

1. Have the children decide which of the following show that God comes first in our lives: **(a) Going to church on Sunday or staying home to watch cartoons. (b) Eating a cookie yourself or sharing it. (c) Saying your prayers before bedtime or deciding you are too tired to pray.**
2. **How do we show that God is important in our lives?** (By acting as images of God in all we "think, and say, and do".)

Extending the Lesson

Art and Craft Projects

Materials Needed

A. Construction paper, markers, scissors, stapler.

B. Half-pint milk cartons, construction paper, glue, stapler, scissors.

C. Pattern for praying hands, yarn, hole punch, scissors.

A. Paper Bibs. To make paper bibs, you will need three pieces of construction paper for each child. From one piece of paper, cut strips approximately 2 inches wide by 9 inches long. These strips will be used as the straps. Attach one end of each strip to the top of each of the other two pieces of paper. Write on the front piece "I will build my life with God". On the back piece write "God loves me". Have the children parade around the room wearing the bibs and singing a favorite song. Remind the children that we build our lives with God by learning about Him, praying to Him, worshiping Him, and by acting as images of God in all we "think, and say, and do".

B. House on the Rock. Give each child a half-pint milk carton. Have the children glue small pieces of black construction paper around the bottom of the carton. These black pieces will be the "rocks" that the house is built on. Cut a piece of construction paper approximately 3 by 3 inches for the roof. Crease this piece in the center and staple to the peak of the carton. The children may then choose to decorate the house as they wish. You may choose to write on the roof "Build your house with the Lord" or "The wise man built a house on rock" to label this project. Remind the children of the story "The House on the Rock". Ask them what they do to show that they are building their lives with God.

C. Praying Hands. Cut two hands for each child from the pattern provided. Punch holes in the hands as shown on the pattern. Give each child a piece of yarn long enough to lace through the holes, lacing the two hands together. Make sure there is a knot on one end of the yarn. The hands will then be tied together on one side but open on the other side. On the inside of the hands write "I pray to God". Remind the children that all our prayers, sacrifices, and acts of love show that God is important in our lives.

Use this pattern from the special pattern packet.

C.

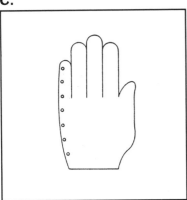

Action Rhyme

> I want God to hear, (*Cup ears.*)
> I want God to see, (*Shade eyes with hands.*)
> That He is most important to me. (*Point to self.*)
> I give Him my prayers, (*Fold hands.*)
> I give Him my love, (*Hands on heart.*)
> I know He watches me from above. (*Shade eyes with hands and look down.*)

Prayer

> *Dear God, I will show that You are first in my life in all I "think, and say, and do". Amen.*

Worksheets

The worksheets can be sent home to be completed or can be completed in the classroom and then sent home. In either case, the worksheets should be used as take-home material because they furnish the basis for parent–child faith discussion.

Pre-school A. Worksheets 33 and 34 relate to the lesson theme and can be distributed to the children after the Application portion of the Lesson Presentation section to reinforce the concept or after the Living the Lesson section to help the children relate the theme to their daily lives.

Pre-school B. Worksheet 85 can be distributed after the Living the Lesson section to help the children relate the theme to their daily lives. Worksheet 86 can be used after the Suggested Story to aid the children's retention of the story.

Kindergarten. Worksheet 54 can be distributed after the Living the Lesson section to help the children relate the theme to their daily lives. Worksheet 55 can be used after its related Suggested Story to aid the children's retention of the story.

Jesus in the Desert

After Jesus was baptized, He wanted to spend some time praying and thinking. He knew it would not be easy to teach all the people about God. Jesus went to the desert all alone to ask His Father's help. He prayed in the desert for forty days and forty nights with very little food to eat or water to drink.

The devil, knowing that Jesus must be hungry, wanted to see if he could tempt Jesus. "If you are God the Son, you can do anything", said the devil. "Why don't you change some of these rocks into bread?"

"I will not", said Jesus. "All people need food for their bodies, but they cannot live without God in their lives."

This did not stop the devil. He tested Jesus again. "If you worship me, I will give you anything you want", the devil said.

"I will not", said Jesus. "God should come first in our lives. God is more important than any riches or treasures on earth. You should love God most of all. Go away, now", commanded Jesus. "You should worship and love only God."

Once more the devil tempted Jesus. Just as before, Jesus would not listen to the devil.

Then the devil went away. The devil knew Jesus would never listen to him or do what he asked.

When Jesus left the desert, He knew He had hard work to do. He wanted to teach everyone that God should come first in their lives.

1. **Where did Jesus go to pray?** (The desert.)
2. **How long was Jesus in the desert?** (Forty days.)
3. **What did Jesus have to eat and drink?** (Very little food and water.)
4. **Who tried to tempt Jesus?** (The devil.)
5. **Did Jesus ever listen to the devil and do what he asked?** (No.)
6. **Would Jesus ever listen to the devil and do what he asked?** (No.)
7. **What did Jesus say we need more than food or treasures?** (God in our lives.)

The House on the Rock

One day two men were building their houses by a river. The first man was very wise. He knew it was important to build a strong house to keep him safe. He dug deep into the ground until he found rock.

"This rock will keep my house strong", he said. "It will protect me."

The second man was foolish. He thought it was more important to have a fancy house. Quickly, he built his house on the sand.

"Look at my house", he said to the wise man. "It is the prettiest house of all. Now I can sit and relax while you work."

The wise man did not stop his work. When his house was all done, it was not the prettiest house, but it was strong. It would protect him.

Soon it began to rain. The rain fell harder and harder. The wind began to blow. The river rose higher and higher. Soon waves were crashing against the wise man's house, but the house stood strong and firm.

Then the waves crashed against the foolish man's house. There was nothing to keep it strong. The river washed away the sand. With one loud splash, the foolish man's house fell into the water!

Jesus said we can be like the house on the rock. If we build our lives with God, He will protect us and keep us safe. We do not need the best toys, or the most money, or the prettiest clothes to be happy here on earth and to go to heaven. We need God in our lives. We show God we want to build our lives with Him by learning about Him, by praying to Him, and by acting as images of God in all we "think, and say, and do".

Review Questions

1. **Where did the wise man build his house?** (On the rock.)
2. **Where did the foolish man build his house?** (On the sand.)
3. **What was most important to the foolish man?** (A fancy house.)
4. **What was important to the wise man?** (A house that would keep him safe.
5. **What happened to the houses when it rained?** (The wise man's house stood firm, and the foolish man's house fell into the water.)
6. **Which house should we be like?** (The wise man's.)
7. **With Whom should we build our lives?** (God.)

Lesson 17

God Cares for Us and All He Has Made

Lesson Focus

We believe that God is the source of all we have and all we need. He loves us. He wants to share His life with us now, and He wants us to be with Him someday in heaven. God has told us, shown us, and given us all that we need to be the best images of God we can be. "If God can clothe in such splendor the grass of the field . . . will He not provide much more for you?" (Matthew 6:30).

In this lesson guardian angels are introduced. God gave each of us a guardian angel to aid us. The vocabulary word is **guardian angel**. A guardian angel is given to each of us by God. Our guardian angels help us to make right choices.

Concepts of Faith

Who takes care of us always?

God takes care of us always.

Whom did God give to each one of us to help and guide us?

God gave each one of us a guardian angel to help and guide us.

Lesson Presentation

Application

Explain to the children that angels are persons, but we cannot see them. They are made in the image of God, as we are. They can think and choose, as we can. But they do not have bodies. They live in heaven with God.

Remind the children of the angels they are familiar with through Bible stories: God sent the angel Gabriel to Mary; an angel appeared to Joseph in a dream; an angel told the shepherds of the birth of Jesus; and an angel told the women that Jesus had risen from the dead. Tell the children that God has given each of us an angel, a guardian angel who loves and cares for each of us.

Our guardian angels help us and guide us to make right choices, and they sometimes may even have protected us from physical harm. We say a special prayer to our guardian angels, asking them to be with us and to help us to be the best images of God we can be. Recite the "Guardian Angel" prayer for the children. Then have them repeat the prayer, phrase by phrase, after you.

> *Angel of God,*
> *my guardian dear,*
> *to whom God's love commits me here,*
> *ever this day be at my side,*
> *to light and guard,*
> *to rule and guide. Amen.*

Discussion Questions

1. **Are angels persons?** (Yes.)
2. **Can they think and choose?** (Yes.)
3. **Do they have bodies?** (No.)
4. **Can we see our guardian angels?** (No.)
5. **Who made the angels?** (God.)
6. **How do our guardian angels help us?** (By helping us to make the right choices and to be the best images of God we can be.)

Suggested Stories

A. "The Birds and the Lilies" (based on Matthew 6:26–34)
B. "The Good Shepherd" (based on Matthew 18:10–14, John 10:11–15)

Living the Lesson

Jesus told us that God takes care of all that He has made. We know God loves us, because He made us in His image.

1. **Who feeds all the birds and all the animals?** (We can put out bird food and feed our own pets, but God provides food for all the animals.)
2. **Who takes care of all the plants, flowers, and trees?** (We take care of our own gardens and lawns, but God provides the sun and the rain for all the plants and trees.)
3. **Are we more important to God than the animals and plants?** (Yes.) **How do we know?** (Because God made us in His image.)
4. **Whom did God give to us to help us and guide us?** (Our guardian angels.)
5. **If God cares for all the plants and animals, and if we are more important to God than the plants and animals, does God care for us?** (Yes. God gives us all we need to be happy here on earth and to be happy with Him someday in heaven.)
6. **Who are some of the persons who help take care of us?** (Guardian angels, parents, priests, policemen, firemen, doctors, nurses, teachers, and so forth.)

We should remember to thank God for all He has given us.

Extending the Lesson

Art and Craft Projects

Materials Needed
A. Blue construction paper, stapler or glue, scissors.
B. Sheep mask pattern, stapler, white construction paper, cotton balls, glue, scissors.
C. Butcher paper, tape, crayons.

A. Construction Paper Birds. Each child will need three strips of blue construction paper, two measuring 2 by 9 inches and one measuring 2 by 11 inches. Have the children use one of the shorter strips and the long strip to form two rings. The smaller ring will be the bird's head, and the larger ring will be the bird's body. Secure each ring with staples or tape and join the rings in the same way. Take the remaining 2- by 9-inch strip and cut the two short sides and one long side in a jagged manner. This strip will be the bird's wings. Have the children attach the strip, straight side up, to the bird's body. The children can add eyes, a beak, and feet to their birds. Remind the children of the story "The Birds and the Lilies". Emphasize that if God takes such good care of the birds and the lilies, He will take care of us even more.

B. Sheep Masks. Cut one sheep mask pattern from white construction paper for each child. Have the children glue cotton balls to the upper portion of the mask. Have them draw eyes, a nose, and a mouth on the sheep. Remind the children of the story "The Good Shepherd". Tell them that Jesus is our Good Shepherd. He loves and cares for us always. You may want to retell the story and have the children act it out using their masks.

C. Mural. Tape a large piece of butcher paper to the blackboard. Tell the children that they are going to work together on one picture. It will be a picture of things God has given us. Have the children list things God has given us, for example, angels, sun, moon, stars, clouds, rain, snow, trees, grass, flowers, butterflies, dogs, cats, people. Then have the children decide where on the mural the trees should go, where the flowers should go, and so on. Assign one or two things to each child to draw. When the picture is finished, write "We thank You, God, for all You have given us."

Use this pattern from the special pattern packet.

B.

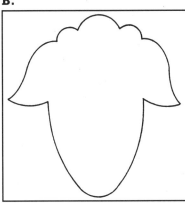

Action Rhyme

> I have a special friend (*Point to self.*)
> That you cannot see. (*Shake head "no".*)
> God sent an angel (*Point to heaven.*)
> To watch over me. (*Then point to self.*)

Prayer

> Dear Lord, You are my Shepherd. Thank You for Your loving care. Amen.

Worksheets

The worksheets can be sent home to be completed or can be completed in the classroom and then sent home. In either case, the worksheets should be used as take-home material because they furnish the basis for parent–child faith discussion.

Pre-school A. Worksheet 35 can be distributed after the Living the Lesson section to help the children relate the theme to their daily lives. Worksheet 36 can be used after the Suggested Story to aid the children's retention of the story.

Pre-school B. Worksheet 87 can be used after the Suggested Story to aid the children's retention of the story. Worksheet 88 can be distributed after the Living the Lesson section to help the children relate the theme to their daily lives.

Kindergarten. Worksheets 56 and 58 can be used after their related Suggested Story to aid the children's retention of the story. Worksheet 57 can be distributed after the Living the Lesson section to help the children relate the theme to their daily lives.

The Birds and the Lilies

One day Jesus was talking to some people in a meadow. Jesus pointed to the birds flying overhead. "Watch the birds in the sky", Jesus said. "God feeds them and takes care of them."

Then Jesus told the people not to worry about having fancy clothes. "Look at the flowers in the field. They do not work. Yet God makes them look beautiful", said Jesus.

Jesus told them that they were more important to God than the birds or the flowers and that God would always take care of them.

We know that God loves and takes care of us, too. God loves us so much He made us in His image. He cares for us by giving us all that we need. He gives us a guardian angel to take care of us. We should thank God for His loving care.

Review Questions

1. **How does God take care of the birds?** (By providing things for them to eat, by providing trees for them to live in, by providing things for them to make nests with, and so forth.)
2. **How does God take care of the flowers in the field?** (By giving them rain and sunshine, and so forth.)
3. **Who did Jesus say are more important to God than the birds and the flowers?** (People are more important.)
4. **Why are we more important to God?** (Because we are made in His image, and the birds and the flowers are not.)
5. **Does God care for us?** (Yes.) **How?** (By giving us families, friends, teachers, priests, guardian angels, and so forth.)

The Good Shepherd

When Jesus lived on earth, people raised sheet in the fields by their homes. People who took care of the sheep were called shepherds. The shepherds were supposed to protect the sheep in case a wolf came close. The shepherds were also supposed to make sure the sheep had enough soft green grass to eat and cool water to drink. Good shepherds liked to take care of their sheep. Jesus told a story about a good shepherd.

This shepherd took good care of his sheep. He knew all their names. He made sure that the sheep lived in a field with green grass and cool streams. The good shepherd enjoyed walking among his sheep. He was always there to protect them from wild animals.

One day something terrible happened. When the good shepherd was walking with his sheep, he noticed that one was missing. "One, two, three . . .", he counted, all the way up to ninety-nine. One sheep was missing!

The good shepherd gathered the rest of the sheep together and closed the gate. Off he went to find his lost sheep. He looked everywhere—in the big field, on the rocky hillside, and behind every bush. The poor little sheep had wandered away. The good shepherd would keep on looking until he found his littlest sheep.

The good shepherd finally found the poor, scared little sheep caught in a thorn bush. He helped the little sheep out and gave him a big hug! The little sheep was happy to be home, and the good shepherd was even happier to have him back.

Jesus said that He is like a good shepherd. He is always willing to stand by us, His sheep, even when we are in trouble. He knows all of us by name, and we belong to His family. He protects us from evil and takes care of us. He was even willing to die for us on the Cross.

Review Questions

1. **What is a shepherd?** (A person who cares for sheep.)
2. **How does a shepherd take care of his sheep?** (Protects them from harm, gives them food and water, loves them, and so forth.)
3. **What happened to one of the good shepherd's sheep?** (It wandered away and got lost.)
4. **What did the good shepherd do?** (Looked everywhere for the little sheep until he found it.)
5. **Who is our Good Shepherd?** (Jesus.)
6. **Does Jesus love us?** (Yes, even when we are in trouble.)

Liturgical and Holiday
Lessons

Lesson 18K   All Saints' Day

Workbook Pages

Pre-school A. 27–28
Pre-school B. 79–80
Kindergarten 42–44

Lesson Focus

This liturgical lesson for kindergarten will introduce the children to All Saints' Day. Explain to the children that on All Saints' Day we remember all the holy men and women who followed Jesus while they were living on earth. They tried always to act as images of God. Now the saints live with God in heaven. We go to Mass and ask the saints to pray for us. The saints are people who lived as images of God on earth and are now living in heaven with God.

Concepts of Faith

Who are the saints?
The saints are people who lived as images of God on earth and are now living in heaven with God.

Lesson Presentation

Application

This lesson contains stories of six saints: Saint John Bosco, Saint Bernadette, Saint Anne, Saint Thérèse, Saint Francis of Assisi, and Saint Nicholas. Read the stories to the children and have them color their workbook pages (found in the kindergarten workbook only).

Living the Lesson

1. Obtain a book containing the meanings of various names. Look up the children's names and tell them what their names mean.
2. Obtain a book of saints' names. Look up the children's names and tell them about their patron saints and when the Church celebrates their feast days.
3. If your parish has a patron saint, look up the life of that saint and tell the children about it.

Extending the Lesson

Art and Craft Project

Materials Needed
Construction paper, stapler, scissors, marker.

Saint's Crown. Make a crown for each child from construction paper. Write the children's names as saints on their crown—for example, Saint Megan, Saint Eric. Tell the children that the saints lived their lives acting as images of God.

Prayer

Dear God, help me to live my life always acting as an image of God, just as Your holy saints did. Amen.

Worksheets

The worksheets can be sent home to be completed or can be completed in the classroom and then sent home. In either case, the worksheets should be used as take-home material because they furnish the basis for parent–child faith discussion.

Kindergarten. Worksheets 59–61 can each be used after its related Suggested Story to aid the children's retention of the story. The pages can be bound together and used as an art and craft project to create a saints book for each child.

Saint John Bosco

As a young boy, John Bosco liked to run and play, laugh, and make jokes. John had many friends because he was so much fun to play with. He never let his friends talk him into doing things that were wrong. If his friends were fighting, John would try to make them stop, because he knew fighting was wrong.

Young John also liked to go to the circus. Sometimes he would put on his own shows for his friends and do tricks he had learned at the circus. After the shows he would talk to his friends about God. He knew that when he grew up he wanted to help many children learn about God.

John's dream came true when he became a priest at the age of 26. He lived at a time when most people were very poor, and there were not many schools. Young boys liked Father John. He found safe places for them to play together. He would teach them how to pray. Some boys had no mothers or fathers and did not have homes to live in. Father John would take care of these boys. Some boys did wrong things, and Father John would talk to them. He would set a good example for them to follow. He would never say "no" to a boy who needed his help.

Saint John Bosco spent his whole life helping young people who were poor or in trouble. He is a special saint for children.

Feast day: January 31

Saint Bernadette

One day a young girl named Bernadette was out getting firewood for her mother. Suddenly, a very beautiful lady appeared in the cave in front of Bernadette. The lady smiled lovingly at Bernadette. She asked Bernadette to pray the Rosary with her.

Bernadette knelt before the lady, and slowly they prayed together. The lady asked Bernadette to come to the spot again soon so they could talk together. Bernadette saw the lady many times. Bernadette asked the lady who she was and what she wanted her to do. The lady said she was the Blessed Mother, Mary. Mary wanted Bernadette to pray the Rosary for sinners. Bernadette loved Mary very much and was happy to do what she asked.

Many people followed Bernadette to the place where Mary appeared. They could not see Mary, but they prayed at that special place. One day, Mary asked Bernadette to dig in the ground. When Bernadette did this, a little river began to come from the dry ground.

Today many people travel to the special place where Mary, the Mother of God, visited little Bernadette. These people pray the Rosary, asking God to help them.

Feast day: February 18

Saint Anne

Saint Anne was the mother of Mary and the grandmother of Jesus.

Anne and her husband, Joachim, lived in a town called Nazareth. Anne did many things—she cooked, washed clothes, and cleaned house. Anne did these things as well as she could, because she loved God and she loved Joachim. While Anne worked, she prayed. Anne and Joachim loved God and each other very much. They were both very sad, because they did not have any children. They prayed to God for many years for a child. Finally, an angel came to them and said that God would give them a daughter. Anne was so happy! When Anne's baby, Mary, was born, Anne thanked God for giving Mary to her and Joachim.

Mary was always cheerful. Without complaining, she did everything that her mother and father wanted her to do. Anne showed Mary how to cook, clean, and sew, just like all the other young girls of Nazareth. Anne taught her daughter to pray to God and to be kind to everyone.

By being a good mother to Mary, Anne helped her to be ready to become the Mother of Jesus. Saint Anne was a very special grandmother.

Feast day: July 26

Saint Thérèse

Many holy people have become saints in heaven by giving up big things and doing very hard things. There was once a little girl who spent her whole life doing little things for others. Her name was Thérèse.

As a little girl, Thérèse was not much different from little girls today. It was often very hard for her to share with her sisters or not be angry with them. She decided she could show her love for God by doing little things that were good for Him and for others, including her sisters. She pleased God by not saying mean things or complaining. Thérèse liked to do many kind little things for people without telling anyone. Thérèse was a quiet little girl. Sometimes her friends were not kind. Thérèse was able to be kind to them with a smile, because she loved God so much. Very often, Thérèse was sick and suffered much pain. She never grumbled. Thérèse would simply say prayers to God and ask Him to help her.

Saint Thérèse always tried to be the best image of God she could be.

Feast day: October 1

Saint Francis of Assisi

Francis lived many years ago in a faraway country. Francis' family was very rich. They lived in a beautiful house, wore beautiful clothes, and always had lots of good food to eat. Francis had many friends. He spent his father's money eating and drinking and having good times with his friends. One day he became sick and had time to think. He decided that he wanted to do good things for God. So he gave all his money and even his clothes back to his father.

Francis liked animals very much. He knew that God made the animals. Animals were not afraid of Francis. One day a wolf was scaring the people in a town. Francis told the wolf to stop frightening the people. The wolf listened to Francis and peacefully followed him into the town. All the people of the town gathered around Francis and the wolf. Francis shook the wolf's paw. The people were no longer afraid and gave the wolf food to eat. The wolf never scared anyone again.

Saint Francis chose to spend his life helping the sick and poor people and telling them about God.

Feast day: October 4

Saint Nicholas

Nicholas was a rich young man. He loved God very much and wanted to help poor people. He knew that they were made in the image of God and that they really needed his help. One day he heard about a man with three daughters who was very, very poor. The poor man was going to send his daughters out into the streets to beg for money. Nicholas knew this would be very hard for the girls to do. So one night Nicholas quietly went to the poor man's house and threw a bag of gold through the open window. Nicholas did not think it was important for the poor family to know his name. The only thing that mattered to Nicholas was that he was able to help them. The daughters did not have to go out to beg, because Nicholas had helped them. Nicholas secretly watched the family and, when they needed help again, he gave them more money. The father and his daughters were happy, but Nicholas was also very happy, because he was sharing with others as he knew God wanted.

During Christmas, we give gifts to other people as Saint Nicholas did many years ago.

Feast day: December 6

Lesson 19   **Thanksgiving**

Workbook Pages
Pre-school A. 37–38
Pre-school B. 89
Kindergarten 62

Lesson Focus

The act of giving thanks is an important part of our spiritual life. However, at Thanksgiving children are often more aware of the table laden with good food and special treats, or of the arrival of friends and relatives, than the true meaning of Thanksgiving. Thanksgiving is a day of giving thanks to God for all He has given us.

It should be emphasized that Thanksgiving is not just a time for a big meal with family and friends. It is a time for all God's family to join together to say "thank you" and to give praise to our loving Father, Who made all things.

Lesson Presentation

Application

Ask the children what Thanksgiving Day means to them. They may say such things as Pilgrims, turkey, pumpkin pie, or going to grandmother's house. Explain to them that these things remind us of Thanksgiving, but there is more to the Thanksgiving holiday. It is a special day of giving thanks—saying "thank you"—to God for all that He has given us. We should thank God every day when we pray. We can make every day a thanksgiving day.

Tell the children that they will be learning a prayer to say before meals. Say the "Blessing before Meals" for the children:

> *Bless us, O Lord, and these Thy gifts,*
> *which we are about to receive from Thy bounty,*
> *through Christ, our Lord. Amen.*

Tell the children that this is a prayer of thanks. When we say this prayer, we are asking God to bless us and our food, and we are thanking Him for the food we are going to share.

Have the children repeat the "Blessing before Meals", phrase by phrase, after you.

Discussion Questions

1. **What should we do on Thanksgiving?** (We should remember to say "thank you" to God for all He has given us, and we should praise Him for all His goodness.)
2. **Should we give thanks to God only on Thanksgiving Day?** (No, we should say "thank you" to God every day.)
3. **How do we thank God?** (In our prayers.)
4. **What prayer do we say before meals?** (The "Blessing before Meals".)

Suggested Story

"Only One Man Said 'Thank You' " (based on Luke 17:11–19)

Living the Lesson

Through our prayers, we thank God for all He has given us. We also show God we are thankful by taking care of what He has given us.

1. **How do we show God we are thankful for our friends?** (By being kind to our friends; by doing nice things for them; by helping them be the best images of God they can be; by praying for them; and so forth.)
2. **How do we show God we are thankful that He made us?** (By taking care of our bodies and not doing anything to harm ourselves; by staying away from people who want us to do wrong things; by reflecting God in all we "think, and say, and do"; and so forth.)
3. **When we litter, or waste things like food, water, or energy, are we showing that we are thankful?** (No, we should take care of the things God has given us.)
4. Remind the children that saying "thank you" is important. We should tell our parents, friends, and others "thank you" for caring for us. We should say "thank you" whenever someone gives us something or does something nice for us.

Extending the Lesson

Art and Craft Projects

Materials Needed
　A. Paper plates, construction paper, glue, magazines, scissors.
　B. Glue, large piece of poster board, magazines, scissors.

A. Paper Plate Turkey. Have the children cut "feathers" from various colors of construction paper. Give each child a paper plate. Using the paper plate as the body of the turkey, have the children glue the "feathers" around the outside edge of the plate. Draw a turkey face in the center of the plate. Cut pictures from magazines of things God has given us and glue a picture on each feather. Or have the children draw a picture on each feather of something God has given us. Remind the children that Thanksgiving is a day to give thanks and praise to God for all that He has given us.

B. Thanksgiving Collage. Have the children draw pictures or cut pictures from magazines of things they are thankful for. Glue the pictures on a large piece of poster board. Hang it in a place where all the children can see it. Invite another class to participate in a Thanksgiving celebration. Make popcorn or ask the children to bring fresh fruit to share with the other class. Before sharing the treats, say the "Blessing before Meals" that the children have learned and ask them to name one thing they are thankful for.

Action Rhyme

> For the sun that gives us light, (*Make circle with arms.*)
> Lord, we thank You. (*Hands folded in prayer.*)
> For the stars that shine at night, (*Wiggle fingers.*)
> Lord, we thank You. (*Hands folded in prayer.*)
> For people here and there, (*Point to others.*)
> Lord, we thank You. (*Hands folded in prayer.*)
> For all the plants and trees, (*With arms over head, sway from side to side.*)
> Lord, we thank You. (*Hands folded in prayer.*)
> For everything we need, (*Arms spread wide.*)
> Lord, we thank You. (*Hands folded in prayer.*)

Prayer

> *Dear God, we thank You today and every day for all that You have given us. Amen.*

Worksheets

The worksheets can be sent home to be completed or can be completed in the classroom and then sent home. In either case, the worksheets should be used as take-home material because they furnish the basis for parent–child faith discussion.

Pre-school A. Worksheet 37 can be distributed after the Living the Lesson section to help the children relate the theme to their daily lives. Worksheet 38 can be used after the Suggested Story to aid the children's retention of the story.

Pre-school B. Worksheet 89 relates to the lesson theme and can be distributed to the children after the Application portion of the Lesson Presentation section to reinforce the concept.

Kindergarten. Worksheet 62 relates to the lesson theme and can be distributed to the children after the Application portion of the Lesson Presentation section to reinforce the concept or after the Living the Lesson section to help the children relate the theme to their daily lives.

Only One Man Said "Thank You"

This is a story that happened long ago, when Jesus lived on earth.

One day ten men were walking along a road. These men were called lepers, because they had a certain kind of sickness. They had many sores that would not heal. Some people were afraid of the lepers because they thought that, if the lepers touched them, they would get the sickness too. The lepers had to live outside the town. The lepers could not live with their families and friends, so they lived together.

The ten lepers saw some people walking down the road. "That is Jesus and His friends", one of the lepers said. "He can make us well again." The lepers waved to Jesus, but He did not see them. So they began to call to Jesus.

"Jesus! Jesus!" they called together. "Please help us!"

Jesus was not afraid when He saw the lepers. He went up to them. "Go and show yourselves to the people in the temple", He said.

As the lepers left for the temple, their sores disappeared! "Look! Jesus has made us well! Now we can go home to our families", said the lepers. Away they hurried, all but one.

One man did not hurry home. He wanted to thank Jesus. He ran to find Jesus. "Thank you", he said, kneeling at Jesus' feet. "You have made me well."

Jesus said, "I made ten men well, and only one has come to thank me. You have pleased me by remembering to say 'thank you'. Go home now and live with your family."

Only one leper remembered to say "thank you" to Jesus. The other nine lepers forgot to thank Jesus. We should try to remember to thank others the way the one leper thanked Jesus. Every day we should give thanks to God for all He has given us.

Review Questions

1. **Why did lepers not live with their families?** (They had a sickness.)
2. **How many lepers called to Jesus?** (Ten lepers.)
3. **What did the lepers ask Jesus to do?** (Help them.)
4. **What did Jesus do?** (He told them to show themselves to the people at the temple.)
5. **Then what happened?** (The lepers were made well.)
6. **How many men were cured?** (Ten.)
7. **How many men remembered to say "thank you" to Jesus?** (Only one.)
8. **What should we remember to say to others and to God?** ("Thank you.")

Lesson 20   # Advent (1)—Preparing Our Hearts and Homes

Workbook Pages
Pre-school A. 39–40
Pre-school B. 90–91
Kindergarten 63–64

Lesson Focus

The season of Advent is a time of waiting and preparing for the celebration of Jesus' birth. Often our materialism interferes with the true meaning of Christmas. Therefore, it is essential for the children to understand that God loved us so much that He sent His own Son, Jesus, God the Son, to us. The children should also understand that Christmas is a celebration of God's love, the same love Jesus wants us to show in our daily lives.

Because children have a difficult time waiting for Christmas, it is important to include them in the preparations and activities of Advent, thus making them more aware of the true meaning of Christmas. Jesus became Man to teach us how to live and love as God intended. He will come again at the end of time to fulfill our hopes.

Our vocabulary word is **Advent**—the time of waiting and getting ready to celebrate Jesus' birthday.

Concepts of Faith

Who is Jesus?
Jesus is God the Son.

When do we celebrate Jesus' birthday?
We celebrate Jesus' birthday on Christmas.

Lesson Presentation

Application

The concept of waiting is illustrated in the explanation of the Advent wreath. Tell the children that a special item is used to count the weeks until Jesus' birthday. It is called an Advent wreath. You may want to show the children an Advent wreath. The wreath is in the shape of a circle, which is a sign that God's love is never ending. The wreath has four candles to count the weeks until Christmas. The candles remind us of the love God has for us and the love we share with others, of the peace we offer each other, of the joy we feel at Jesus' birthday, and of the hope for heaven that Jesus brings.

It is suggested that a "living" Advent wreath be used weekly during Advent. To form a "living" Advent wreath, choose four children to represent the candles. One pink and three purple aprons made from construction paper can be draped from the children's shoulders.

To make aprons, tape two pieces of construction paper together. Attach two strips of paper at the top of these pieces to form the straps. Tape two more pieces of construction paper together and fasten them to the other end of the straps. Slip this apron over the child's head.

Have the remaining children form a circle around the "candles" to simulate a wreath. (These children can hold onto a long piece of green ribbon or a long strip of green crepe paper to simulate a wreath.) On the first week one purple "candle" is "lit": the child holds a construction paper "flame" overhead. On each succeeding week an additional candle is lit. (The pink one is the third to be lit.) A short explanation of the significance of each candle (love, peace, joy, and hope) should precede the "lighting" (handing out) of the flames. You may choose to have the wreath move in a circle around the candles as the children sing an Advent song. A short prayer should be recited before the flame is "blown out" (taken away).

While not stressing the idea of Santa Claus, we can use his popularity to emphasize the true meaning of Christmas. The children will undoubtedly mention Santa at some time during Advent. When they do, ask them why Santa brings gifts to children. After they have responded, explain that Santa loves Jesus very much. Because of his love for Jesus, he wants everyone to share in the happiness of Jesus' birthday. So Santa gives us gifts.

It should be stressed that Jesus is the best gift of all. Jesus, God the Son, is a gift of love to us from God the Father.

Discussion Questions

1. **What do we call the time before Christmas?** (Advent.)
2. **What do we use to count the weeks until Christmas?** (An Advent wreath.)
3. **How many candles are on the Advent wreath?** (Four, three purple and one pink.)
4. **What do the candles stand for?** (Love, peace, joy, and hope.)
5. **When is Jesus' birthday?** (Christmas is Jesus" birthday.)
6. **Who is Jesus?** (Jesus is God the Son.)

Living the Lesson

As we wait for the celebration of Jesus' birthday, Christmas, we prepare our homes and, more important, our hearts. During the waiting period, Advent, there are many ways in which we can show our love for God and others. It is important that we share the true meaning of Christmas, that is, love, in our daily lives throughout the entire year and not just during this season.

1. **What are some things we wait for?** (Buses, birthdays, friends to come, our turn to be first, new babies.)
2. **Is it easy to wait for things?** (No, it is hard.)
3. **What are some of the signs we see and hear while we wait for Christmas?** (We hear Christmas songs. We see decorations, Christmas trees, Advent wreaths, and so forth.)
4. **How do we prepare our hearts during Advent?** (Saying prayers, going to church, being good, sharing gifts of love, and so forth.)
5. **How do we prepare our homes?** (Putting up Nativity scenes, making cookies, putting up decorations and trees, wrapping presents, and so forth.)

6. **What is the most important thing about Christmas: cookies, gifts, company, Santa, or Jesus' birthday?** (Jesus' birthday.)

7. **How can we share our love at Christmas time?** (By being extra helpful, making something for someone, special hugs, forgiving someone, and so forth.)

Extending the Lesson

Art and Craft Projects

Materials Needed

   A. Construction paper (green, purple, pink, and red), wreath pattern, stapler, glue.

   B. Red and green construction paper, glue, stapler.

   C. Calendar page of December (blank), pencil, Nativity sticker.

   A. Advent Wreath. Make an Advent wreath following the pattern provided. Before starting this project, it is important that the children understand the reason for an Advent wreath. Tell the children that during Advent we see many things to remind us that Jesus' birthday is near. We make Advent wreaths to count the weeks until Jesus' birthday. As the children glue a flame to each candle, they will know Christmas is near.

   B. Advent Chain. Make an Advent chain for each child by cutting enough construction paper strips so that one may be removed each day. Glue or staple the strips together to form a chain. Cut a large star to be fastened to the top of the chain. Explain to the children that the chain will help them count the days until Christmas. Tell the children to remove one link of the chain each night before they go to bed. When they remove the link, they should say a special prayer asking God to help them act as images of God or thanking God the Father for His wonderful gift of love, Jesus, God the Son.

   C. Advent Calendar. Give each child a copy of a blank calendar page for December. Make a sample for them and have them write the dates on the calendar. Remark how long the wait during Advent seems. Have the children paste the Nativity sticker on the 25th. Tell the children that Christmas is Jesus' birthday. Have the children color a square each day until Christmas. Remind them to ask God every day to help them act as images of God not only during Advent, but always.

Action Rhyme

Let's count the days till Christmas (*Point as if counting.*)
And say a prayer each day (*Fold hands in prayer.*)
To show our love for Jesus (*Hands on heart.*)
In a special way.
Jesus was born on Christmas (*Pretend to rock a baby in arms.*)
And everyone should know (*Point to others.*)
That Jesus came to save us
Because He loves us so. (*Hug self.*)

Use this pattern from the special pattern packet.

A.

Prayer

Come, Lord Jesus,
help prepare our hearts and homes for Your birthday.
Amen.

Worksheets

The worksheets can be sent home to be completed or can be completed in the classroom and then sent home. In either case, the worksheets should be used as take-home material because they furnish the basis for parent–child faith discussion.

Pre-school A. Worksheet 39 can be distributed after the Living the Lesson section to help the children relate the theme to their daily lives. Worksheet 40 relates to the lesson theme and can be distributed to the children after the Application portion of the Lesson Presentation to reinforce the concept.

Pre-school B. Worksheet 90 can be distributed after the Living the Lesson section to help the children relate the theme to their daily lives. Worksheet 91 relates to the lesson theme and can be distributed to the children after the Application portion of the Lesson Presentation to reinforce the concept.

Kindergarten. Worksheet 63 can be distributed after the Living the Lesson section to help the children relate the theme to their daily lives. Worksheet 64 relates to the lesson theme and can be distributed to the children after the Application portion of the Lesson Presentation to reinforce the concept.

Lesson 21 — Advent (2)—Mary Said "Yes" to God

Workbook Pages

Pre-school A. 41–42

Pre-school B. 92–93

Kindergarten 65–66

Lesson Focus

In this lesson we will introduce Mary as the Mother of God. She is an example to all of us. God chose Mary to be the mother of our Savior, Jesus. Her heart was always full of love for God. Hence, when the angel appeared to Mary and asked her to be the mother of Jesus, Mary said "yes" to God. God helped Mary as she prepared her heart and her home for Jesus' birth. After His birth she loved and cared for Jesus in the same ways our mothers love and care for us. She is our loving mother, who intercedes for us at the throne of God.

It is important that the children learn that Mary is the Mother of God. To introduce this, tell the children that Mary is the mother of Jesus. Then ask the children who Jesus is. They should respond that Jesus is God the Son. At that point, lead the children to the conclusion that Mary is the Mother of God. Say to them, "If Jesus is God the Son and Mary is the mother of Jesus, then Mary is the Mother of _____." (Have the children supply the word "God".)

Concepts of Faith

Who is Mary?

Mary is the Mother of God.

Lesson Presentation

Explain to the children that today they are going to learn a new prayer—a prayer to Jesus' mother, a prayer to Mary.

The prayer starts with **Hail, Mary.** That is like saying, "Hello, Mary."

The prayer goes on to say: **full of grace.** We know that grace is God's own life. So this means that Mary was full of God's own life.

Next we say: **the Lord is with thee.** This means that Mary never sinned. She never made wrong choices that would have displeased God. She always acted as an image of God.

Blessed art thou amongst women. There are many good and famous women, but Mary is the best of all.

Blessed is the fruit of thy womb, Jesus. Mary was to be the mother of Jesus.

Holy Mary, Mother of God. Mary is the mother of Jesus. Jesus is God the Son. So Mary is the Mother of God.

Pray for us sinners. Because Mary is the Mother of God, He loves her very much, just as we love our moms very much. God hears Mary's prayers, and we ask her to pray for us.

Now and at the hour of our death. Amen. We ask Mary to pray for us so that we will always act as images of God. Then, when we die, we will be happy in heaven with Jesus and His mother.

Slowly say the whole prayer again, this time without the explanations, so the children can hear the words. Then have the children repeat each phrase after you.

Discussion Questions

1. **Why do we honor Mary?** (Because she is the Mother of God.)
2. **What is the name of the special prayer we say to Mary?** (The "Hail Mary".)
3. **Can we call Mary, the Mother of God, our mother, too?** (Yes, because we are made in the image of God.)

Suggested Story

"Mary Said 'Yes' to God" (based on Luke 1:26–45)

Living the Lesson

Mary willingly chose to do what God asked her to do. Mary is an example for all people. She showed her love for God in all she "thought, and said, and did". We should follow her example. We ask Mary to pray for all of us so we will be more like her and her Son, Jesus.

1. **Mary took care of Jesus, as our mothers take care of us. How do we show our love for our mothers?** (Being good, setting the table, picking up our toys, giving her hugs and kisses, saying "I love you", and so forth.)
2. **How can we show Mary we love her?** (By praying to her; by being like her—that is, by being the best images of God we can be; by loving her Son, Jesus, and so forth.)
3. **Can we ask Mary to pray for us?** (Yes, she loves us because God made us in His image.)
4. **Why do we pray to Mary?** (Because she is the Mother of God and He loves her very much. We ask Mary to pray for us, and God listens to her prayers.)

Extending the Lesson

Art and Craft Projects

Materials Needed

   A. Paper plates, blue tissue paper, stapler, construction paper, scissors.

   B. Doilies, construction paper, gold pipe cleaners, stapler, glue, cardboard tube from paper products.

   A. Paper Plate Figure of Mary. Divide a paper plate into four equal sections. Cut one section from the paper plate and fold the plate into a cone shape. Secure it with a staple. Cut a circle from construction paper for Mary's head. Have the children add the facial features. Tape or staple the head at the neck to the pointed end of the cone. Cut a pie-shaped piece of blue tissue paper for Mary's veil. Tape or staple the veil to the top of the head. Remind the children that Mary is the Mother of God. She is our mother, too.

B. Angel Gabriel Figure. Using a cardboard tube (such as from a roll of paper towels or wax paper), cut a 5-inch length and cover it with white paper (for the angel's body). Gather a doily in the center and staple it to the tube to form wings. Cut a small circle from construction paper for the angel's face. Have the children fill in the features. Form a halo from a gold pipe cleaner—making a small circle on one end, leaving the remainder straight. Position the halo over the angel's head and attach the pipe cleaner to the back of the angel's body. Ask the children how they would feel if an angel appeared to them. Emphasize the willingness of Mary to please God by doing what He asked. Explain that an angel is a messenger of God.

Action Rhyme

> An angel came to Mary, (*Hands over head like a halo.*)
> And said, "God has chosen you (*Point.*)
> "To have a special baby, (*Cradle arms.*)
> "Because your love is true. (*Hands on heart.*)
> "You will call Him Jesus,
> "And everyone will know, (*Open arms wide.*)
> "He's a special gift from God,
> "Because He loves us so." (*Hug self.*)

Prayer

> *Dear God, help me to be like Jesus' mother, Mary, and do what pleases You. Amen.*

Worksheets

The worksheets can be sent home to be completed or can be completed in the classroom and then sent home. In either case, the worksheets should be used as take-home material because they furnish the basis for parent–child faith discussion.

Pre-school A. Worksheet 41 can be used after the Suggested Story to aid the children's retention of the story. Worksheet 42 can be distributed after the Living the Lesson section to help the children relate the theme to their daily lives.

Pre-school B. Worksheet 92 can be used after the Living the Lesson section to help the children relate the theme to their daily lives. Worksheet 93 can be used after the Suggested Story to aid the children's retention of the story.

Kindergarten. Worksheet 65 can be distributed after the Living the Lesson section to help the children relate the theme to their daily lives. Worksheet 66 can be used after the Suggested Story to aid the children's retention of the story.

Mary Said "Yes" to God

When the right time had come, God sent His angel Gabriel to a town called Nazareth. Gabriel went to visit a young woman named Mary. He had something very important to ask Mary. Gabriel greeted Mary warmly, saying, "Hail, Mary, full of grace. The Lord is with you. Blessed are you among women."

At first Mary was afraid. She did not understand what the angel was saying.

Then Gabriel said, "Do not be afraid, Mary. I have come to bring you wonderful news. God has a special plan for you. Soon you will have a son. You will name Him Jesus. He will be the Savior of the world." Then Gabriel said, "So you will know that what I say will come true, I will tell you that your cousin Elizabeth is also going to have a baby."

Mary did not know how all this could happen to her. But she knew that she would lovingly do what God wanted. She said to the angel, "I will do whatever God asks. Let it happen to me as you said."

When the angel disappeared, Mary knelt down and prayed to God. She offered God all her love. She felt happy to be chosen by God for such a special plan. The next day, Mary went to see Elizabeth. When Elizabeth saw Mary coming, she came out to meet her.

Elizabeth said to her, "Blessed are you among women, and blessed is the fruit of your womb."

Mary and Elizabeth were both happy about the wonderful plan God had for them. Elizabeth's baby would grow up to be John the Baptist. Mary's Son would be the Savior of the world.

Review Questions

1. **Who appeared to Mary?** (An angel.)
2. **What was the angel's name?** (Gabriel.)
3. **How did Mary feel when the angel appeared to her?** (Afraid.)
4. **What important question did the angel ask Mary?** (Would she do what God wanted and be the mother of Jesus?)
5. **Did Mary do what God wanted?** (Yes.)
6. **Who else was going to have a baby?** (Mary's cousin Elizabeth.)
7. **Who would Elizabeth's baby grow up to be?** (John the Baptist.)
8. **Who was Mary's baby?** (Jesus, God the Son.)

Advent (3)—Joseph, Jesus' Father on Earth

Workbook Pages
Pre-school A. 43–44
Pre-school B. 94–95
Kindergarten 67–68

Lesson Emphasis

Joseph received special graces from God to be the head of the Holy Family. He was chosen by God to be Jesus' foster father and Mary's husband. Like Jesus and Mary, Joseph chose to obey the will of God in all things. He cared for Jesus and Mary out of love for them and for God.

The Holy Family found peace and joy through loving and serving God and each other faithfully. They are an example of what our families should be. We pray to Jesus, Mary, and Joseph for our families so that we can find peace and joy. We ask St. Joseph to help all fathers to take good care of their children.

Explain to the children that Joseph took care of Jesus. He acted as Jesus' father on earth.

Concepts of Faith

Who was Joseph?
Joseph was Jesus' father on earth.

Lesson Presentation

Explain to the children that Joseph was an honest and hard-working carpenter who loved God with all his heart and soul. (A carpenter works with wood and makes things from wood.) Joseph felt honored at being asked by God to provide care for Jesus. Joseph knew he would not be Jesus' real father, but he would do all the things for Jesus that our fathers do for us. When an angel appeared to him and asked him to be Jesus' father on earth, Joseph said "yes", showing his faith and love.

We see God's love in our fathers (and other men who care for us). God wants fathers to take good care of their children. We ask St. Joseph to help all fathers to take care of their children.

Discussion Questions

1. **Who was Jesus' father on earth?** (Joseph.)
2. **What was Joseph's job?** (He was a carpenter.)
3. **What does a carpenter do?** (He makes things out of wood.)
4. **Will Joseph help all fathers to love their families?** (Yes, fathers pray to him for his help.)

Suggested Story

"Joseph's Special Dream" (based on Matthew 1:18–25, Luke 2:1)

Living the Lesson

1. **How did Joseph care for Jesus?** (He gave Jesus food and clothing. He taught Jesus how to make things out of wood. Most of all, he loved Jesus.)
2. **What do you think Joseph and Jesus did together?** (Played games, made things, went on walks, helped Mary, and so forth.)
3. **How is Joseph like our fathers?** (Our fathers love us, take care of us, work hard, and so forth.)
4. **How can we show our love for our fathers?** (Help them, give them hugs, say "I love you", and so forth.)

Extending the Lesson

Art and Craft Projects

Materials Needed
   A. Paper plates, construction paper, glue, stapler, brown or black yarn, scissors.
   B. Craft sticks, paper, glue, crayons.

   A. Paper Plate Figure of Joseph. Divide a paper plate into four equal sections. Cut one section from the paper plate. Form the paper plate into a cone shape. Secure it with a staple. Cut a small circle from construction paper for Joseph's head. Have the children add the facial features. Brown or black yarn can be cut and glued into place for hair and beard. Attach the head to the top of the cone. Cut a pie-shaped piece of construction paper for Joseph's robe and have the children color it. Attach the robe to the cone figure. Remind the children that Joseph was Jesus' father on earth.
   B. Picture Frame. Have the children draw a Christmas picture. Remind them that Joseph was a carpenter and made things out of wood. They will make a picture frame out of wood, just as Joseph did. After they have finished their pictures, have the children glue craft sticks around the pictures. If they wish, they can decorate the frames. Tell them they can each give their pictures to someone as a Christmas present.

Action Rhyme

> Joseph hammered, Joseph sawed. (*Motions to fit words.*)
> He worked hard each day. (*Wipe brow with hand.*)
> He showed his love for God,
> And thanked God as he prayed. (*Fold hands.*)
> He took care of Jesus (*Cradle arms.*)
> Because God asked him to,
> Just as your own daddy
> Takes good care of you. (*Cradle arms.*)

Prayer

> *Thank you, St. Joseph, for taking care of Mary and Jesus.*
> *Please take care of us, too. Amen.*

Worksheets

The worksheets can be sent home to be completed or can be completed in the classroom and then sent home. In either case, the worksheets should be used as take-home material because they furnish the basis for parent–child faith discussion.

Pre-school A. Worksheet 43 can be distributed after the Living the Lesson section to help the children relate the theme to their daily lives. Worksheet 44 relates to the lesson theme and can be distributed to the children after the Application portion of the Lesson Presentation to reinforce the concept.

Pre-school B. Worksheet 94 relates to the lesson theme and can be distributed to the children after the Application portion of the Lesson Presentation, to reinforce the concept. Worksheet 95 can be used after the Suggested Story to aid the children's retention of the story.

Kindergarten. Worksheets 67 and 68 relate to the lesson theme and can be distributed to the children after the Application portion of the Lesson Presentation to reinforce the concept.

Joseph's Special Dream

Joseph lived in a town called Nazareth. He was a carpenter. He made things out of wood for people. The people in the town knew that Joseph was a good carpenter and a good man. They knew that Joseph loved God very much.

Joseph was planning to marry a young woman named Mary. He loved her very much. One day, Mary surprised Joseph by telling him she was going to have a baby. Joseph wondered about that. Then one night, while Joseph was sleeping, an angel appeared to him in a dream. The angel said, "Do not be afraid. Mary is going to have a special baby. You are to name Him Jesus. He will help all the people." Joseph believed the angel and promised to take care of Mary and Jesus.

Mary and Joseph loved each other very much. They both loved God very much, too. They waited happily for Jesus to be born.

One day some neighbors told Joseph that the king wanted to count all the people. All had to go to the town where their families came from. Joseph had to go to Bethlehem to be counted. It was then close to the time when Mary's baby was to be born. Joseph did not want to leave Mary, and Mary did not want Joseph to travel alone. So they decided to go to Bethlehem together.

In those days there were no cars or trains or planes. Most of the time, people walked wherever they went. But Joseph had a donkey. Mary rode on the donkey, and Joseph walked alongside. It was a long way to Bethlehem.

Because all the people had to be counted, the roads were very crowded. The town of Bethlehem was very crowded, too. Joseph tried to find a place to stay, but there was no room for them. Joseph was very upset. How could he keep his promise to take care of Mary and the baby Who would soon be born?

Tell the children that they have to wait to hear the rest of the story. Waiting is a part of Advent.

Review Questions

1. **What was Joseph's job?** (Carpenter.)
2. **What was the name of the woman whom Joseph wanted to marry?** (Mary.)
3. **How did Mary surprise Joseph?** (She told him she was going to have a baby.)
4. **Who appeared to Joseph in his dream?** (An angel.)
5. **What did the angel say?** (Do not be afraid. Mary is going to have a special baby. You will name Him Jesus.)
6. **Did Joseph believe the angel?** (Yes.)
7. **What did Joseph promise?** (To take care of Mary and Jesus.)
8. **Where did Joseph and Mary have to go near the time when Jesus would be born?** (To Bethlehem.)

Lesson 23 Advent (4)—Christmas Is Jesus' Birthday

Workbook Pages
Pre-school A. 45–46
Pre-school B. 96–97
Kindergarten 69–70

Lesson Focus

Jesus came to us as an infant. He was conceived by the Holy Spirit, and He was born of the Virgin Mary in a humble stable. From the very first, His mission was to teach us who we are and how we are to act. Through His acts, even as an infant, He reveals to us that we are images of God and also how an image of God acts. Through His death and Resurrection, He makes it possible for us to act as God's images. He teaches us that life is truly a celebration of love to be offered to God. On His birthday, we renew our commitments to a life of love and pray that our hearts be filled with the peace and love of the Christ Child.

It is important for the children to understand that Christmas is a worldwide celebration of love: the love that God has for us, and the love we have for God and others.

We will use **Christmas** as the vocabulary word. Christmas is Jesus' birthday.

Concepts of Faith

What is Christmas?
Christmas is Jesus' birthday.

Lesson Presentation

Application

Show the children the various pieces of a Nativity set. However, do not set the pieces in place as yet. When each piece is presented to the children, ask them what or who it helps us to remember.

Then review the stories from the Advent lessons up to this point.

Discussion Questions

1. **Who is Jesus?** (Jesus is God the Son.)
2. **Who is Jesus' mother?** (Mary.)
3. **Who was Jesus' father on earth?** (Joseph.)

Suggested Story

"Christmas Is Jesus' Birthday" (based on Luke 2:1–18)

Living the Lesson

1. Show the children the Nativity set again. This time, have the children tell the story as you put the pieces in place.
2. **Why do we give gifts at Christmas time?** (To show our love for others. This love for others is a reflection of God's love for us.)
3. **Who is the best gift?** (Jesus, God the Son, is the best gift. He is a gift of love from God the Father to each of us.)
4. Have a birthday celebration by sharing juice and a treat, and by singing Christmas carols. Remember to sing "Happy Birthday" to baby Jesus.

Extending the Lesson

Art and Craft Projects

Materials Needed

A. Poster board, glue, hole punch, crayons, glitter, ribbon or yarn.

B. Half-pint milk cartons, craft sticks, yellow yarn, scissors, glue, construction paper, miniature plastic babies (available from craft stores).

A. Star Decorations. Give each child a star cut from poster board. Write on the star "Happy Birthday, Jesus". Have the children decorate the star with glitter. Punch a hole in one point of each star, and attach a 3-inch loop of yarn or ribbon. The children can then hang their stars on their Christmas trees at home.

B. Milk Carton Manger. Cut off the peaked tops of the half-pint milk cartons (one for each child). Cover this peaked section inside and out with brown construction paper. Make **X**s from the craft sticks. Glue an **X** to each side of the covered carton-tops, to form the legs of a manger. Cut short pieces of yellow yarn and put some in each manger for straw. Give each child a miniature baby to place in the manger. Remind the children that Christmas is a celebration of love: God's love for us and our love for God and others. Christmas is Jesus' birthday.

Action Rhyme

> In a stable (*Hands form peak of roof.*)
> Far away,
> On a special night,
> A very special baby lay, (*Cradle arms.*)
> And a star twinkled bright. (*Wiggle fingers.*)
> Mary and Joseph knelt beside (*Fold hands in prayer.*)
> A very tiny bed,
> Where the little Holy Child (*Cradle arms.*)
> Rested His sweet head. (*Rest cheek on hands.*)

Prayer

> *Happy birthday, Jesus.*
> *Come fill our hearts with Your love and peace.*
> *Amen.*

Worksheets

The worksheets can be sent home to be completed or can be completed in the classroom and then sent home. In either case, the worksheets should be used as take-home material because they furnish the basis for parent–child faith discussion.

Pre-school A. Worksheet 45 relates to the lesson theme and can be distributed to the children after the Application portion of the Lesson Presentation, to reinforce the concept, or after the Living the Lesson section to help the children relate the theme to their daily lives. Worksheet 46 may be used after the Suggested Story to aid the children's retention of the story.

Pre-school B. Worksheet 96 relates to the lesson theme and can be distributed to the children after the Application portion of the Lesson Presentation, to reinforce the concept, or after the Living the lesson section to help the children relate the theme to their daily lives. Worksheet 97 can be used after the Suggested Story to aid the children's retention of the story.

Kindergarten. Worksheet 69 relates to the lesson theme and can be distributed to the children after the Application portion of the Lesson Presentation, to reinforce the concept, or after the Living the Lesson section to help the children relate the theme to their daily lives. Worksheet 70 can be used after the Suggested Story to aid the children's retention of the story.

Christmas Is Jesus' Birthday

Joseph and Mary traveled all the way to Bethlehem to be counted. Bethlehem was very crowded, and there was no place for Joseph and Mary to stay. However, a kind man felt sorry for them and let them stay in his stable overnight. There was clean soft hay in the stable for them to sit on. They would be safe and warm there. Mary and Joseph thanked the man.

That night a wonderful thing happened. Jesus was born! Mary wrapped Him in a blanket. Joseph put some clean hay in a manger, and Mary laid Jesus down in it. Mary and Joseph thanked God for this wonderful baby.

In a field outside of town, some shepherds were taking care of their sheep. Suddenly an angel appeared to them. The angel said, "Do not be afraid. I bring good news! In a stable in Bethlehem, a special baby has been born. He is the Savior of the world." Then the sky filled with angels, all praising God, saying, "Glory to God. Peace on earth."

When the angels went back to heaven, the shepherds said to one another, "Let us go into Bethlehem and see this special baby." They found Mary, Joseph, and the baby Jesus in the stable. The shepherds knelt down and thanked God. They told many people what had happened to them on that wonderful night.

Review Questions

1. **Where was Jesus born?** (In a stable in Bethlehem.)
2. **Who came to see Jesus?** (Shepherds.)
3. **Who told the shepherds about Jesus?** (An angel.)
4. **What did the angels say when they praised God?** (Glory to God. Peace on earth.)

Lesson 24 **Lent**

Workbook Pages
Pre-school A. 47
Pre-school B. 98
Kindergarten 71–72

Lesson Focus

The grace of God given to us first through Baptism makes it possible for us to join our sufferings and sacrifices with the sufferings and sacrifices of Jesus for the redemption of mankind from sin. As baptized Catholics, we also are able to share in the joy of the Resurrection of Jesus on Easter.

During Lent we prepare ourselves for the joy and new life of Easter. We make this preparation as the people of God's family, the Church. We make this preparation by doing what Jesus did. Those in God's family spend time fasting and praying during Lent, just as Jesus spent time fasting and praying in the desert. It is important for the children to understand that our prayers, sacrifices, and acts of love done during Lent show others how important God is in our lives. The Lenten period is a time to renew our baptismal vows, our promises to live as Jesus did.

The vocabulary word is **Lent**. Lent is a time for preparing ourselves for the joy and new life of Easter.

Concepts of Faith

What is Lent?

Lent is a time for preparing ourselves for the joy and new life of Easter.

Lesson Presentation

Application

Even small children can participate in the practices of the Lenten season. It is important that the children be aware of the meaning of Lent, as well as of how we as Catholics prepare ourselves for the joy of Easter. Tell the children that during the forty days of Lent we take more time from our lives to devote to God. Explain that through the season of Lent we show God that He is most important in our lives.

During Lent we make sacrifices to offer to God. We "do without" things such as a favorite television show or treats. We have smaller or simpler meals at home. On the first day of Lent and all the Fridays during Lent, the grownups do not eat meat. During Lent we show God our love by spending more time praying or by going to Mass every day. All of these acts of love we should do willingly without complaining.

Tell the children the Lenten season begins on Ash Wednesday, a special day set aside to show our love for God. We ask God to forgive the wrong choices we have made and to help us not to do wrong again. On Ash Wednesday the parish priest makes the "Sign of the Cross" on our foreheads with ashes. This is a reminder that

God made us from nothing and that nothing on earth is as important as loving God. We want to be the best images of God we can be, so that we can share God's life now, and also so that when we die we will have new life with God in heaven. Explain to the children that it does not hurt when the priest puts ashes on their foreheads, and that the ashes will not last forever. (You may wish to show them what it feels like by making a cross on their foreheads with your thumb.)

Discussion Questions

1. **What do we call the time when we are getting ourselves ready for the joy of Easter?** (Lent.)
2. **How long is Lent?** (Forty days.)
3. **During Lent, what are we showing to be most important in our lives?** (God.)
4. **How do we show that God is important to us?** (By extra prayers, sacrifices—going without things—and acts of love.)
5. **What is the first day of Lent?** (Ash Wednesday.)
6. **On Ash Wednesday, what does the priest put on our foreheads?** (Ashes.)
7. **What do the ashes remind us of?** (That God made us from nothing; that nothing on earth is as important as loving God.)

Living the Lesson

Jesus sacrificed (gave up) His life for us because He loves us. We make sacrifices during Lent to show that we love Jesus and want to act as images of God. Explain sacrifices as doing something good or giving up something to show God we love Him, and that He is most important to us.

1. **What are some things we could give up (not have) during Lent?** (Candy, cookies, a favorite television show, a favorite toy, pop, treats, gum, and so forth.)
2. **Would it be a sacrifice to give up something we do not really like?** (No, a sacrifice is an act of love for God. We give up things we like or do extra things to show how much we love God.)
3. **What are some things we could do during Lent?** (Clean up our rooms, clear the table, dust the furniture, sweep the floor, be nice to our brothers and sisters, say "thank you" to our moms when they make us a meal, and so forth.)

Extending the Lesson

Art and Craft Projects

Materials Needed
   A. **Pre-school.** Construction paper, crayons, scissors.
   B. **Kindergarten.** Coupon from the Kindergarten Workbook.

A. "Cross on the Forehead" Picture. Cut one oval from construction paper for each child. Have the children draw facial features on the oval. Using a black crayon, have the children draw a cross on the foreheads of the drawn faces. Remind the children of the cross the parish priest makes on our foreheads with ashes on Ash Wednesday.

B. Lenten Coupon. Using the coupon from the Kindergarten Workbook, have the children decide what they would like to give up or what they would like to do during Lent to show their love for God. Fill out a coupon for each child. Remind the children that it might be difficult to do these acts of love, but that they will be showing God how much they love Him.

Action Rhyme

I will try
With all my heart (*Nod head "yes".*)
To follow Jesus each day
And give my love to God. (*Hug self.*)
That's the Lenten way.

Prayer

*Dear Lord, we ask You to help us be bright images of God.
We offer You all we "think, say, and do".
Amen.*

Worksheets

The worksheets can be sent home to be completed or can be completed in the classroom and then sent home. In either case, the worksheets should be used as take-home material because they furnish the basis for parent–child faith discussion.

Pre-school A. Worksheet 47 relates to the lesson theme and can be distributed to the children after the Application portion of the Lesson Presentation to reinforce the concept.

Pre-school B. Worksheet 98 relates to the lesson theme and can be distributed to the children after the Application portion of the Lesson Presentation to reinforce the concept.

Kindergarten. Worksheet 71 can be distributed after the Living the Lesson section to help the children relate the theme to their daily lives, or it can be used as suggested in the Arts and Crafts section. Worksheet 72 can be used after the vocabulary word (Lent) has been introduced.

Lesson 25K   Stations of the Cross

Workbook Pages
Kindergarten 73–79

Lesson Focus

This liturgical unit, for kindergarten, is an introduction to the Stations of the Cross. Tell the children that the Stations of the Cross help us remember all that Jesus suffered because He loves us.

Jesus lived, suffered, and died for the redemption of all people. Through His death on the Cross, He freed us from our sins and made it possible for us to share God's grace again.

Concepts of Faith

What do the Stations of the Cross help us to remember?
The Stations of the Cross help us to remember all that Jesus suffered because He loves us.

Lesson Application

Remove the "Stations of the Cross" pages from the kindergarten workbook. As you show the pictures to the children, explain each Station as follows:

1. **Pilate condemns Jesus.**
   Some people did not like Jesus. They did not want Him to teach the people about God. The people who did not like Jesus had some soldiers arrest Jesus. The soldiers hurt Jesus and put a crown of thorns on His head.

2. **Jesus carries His cross.**
   The soldiers gave Jesus a heavy wooden cross to carry. They were taking Him to the hill called Calvary, to execute Him. Jesus carried the cross willingly, even though it was very heavy.

3. **Jesus falls the first time.**
   The cross became heavier and heavier for Jesus to carry. He fell down under its weight, but He got up and carried the cross again.

4. **Jesus meets His mother.**
   Along the way to Calvary, Jesus saw Mary, His mother. He saw how sad she was to see Him suffer.

5. **Simon helps Jesus to carry the cross.**
   The soldiers made a man named Simon help Jesus to carry the cross. Simon was strong. He walked with Jesus and helped Him carry the heavy cross.

6. **Veronica wipes Jesus' face.**
   A woman named Veronica, who loved and believed in Jesus, saw how Jesus suffered. She came out of the crowd to wipe Jesus' face with her veil. A picture of His face remained on the veil.

7. **Jesus falls the second time.**
   It became harder for Jesus to walk, and He fell a second time. But again He got up and continued to carry the cross.

8. **Jesus meets the women of Jerusalem.**
   Along the way, Jesus passed a group of women who were weeping for Him. They were His friends. They loved Him and believed in Him. Jesus told them not to cry for Him.

9. **Jesus falls the third time.**
   A third time, Jesus fell to the ground. He was very tired. But because He loves us, He got up again.

10. **The soldiers take Jesus' clothes.**
    A large crowd of people followed Jesus and the soldiers to Calvary. The soldiers took Jesus' clothes and made fun of Him. They treated Him rudely.

11. **Jesus is nailed to the cross.**
    The soldiers nailed Jesus' hands and feet to the cross. This was very painful for Jesus, but He prayed and asked God to forgive the soldiers.

12. **Jesus dies on the cross.**
    Standing near the cross were Jesus' mother, Mary, and His Apostle John. Mary saw how terribly Jesus suffered and shared His suffering herself. Jesus asked John to take care of Mary. And then Jesus died on the cross, so that by His sacrifice all people could share God's life again.

13. **Jesus is taken down from the cross.**
    After Jesus died, the soldiers let His friends take His body down from the cross. Mary held her Son's head on her lap. She was very sad. All the other friends of Jesus were very sad, too.

14. **Jesus is placed in the tomb.**
    Some of Jesus' friends prepared His body for burial. They wrapped it in a clean cloth and placed it in a tomb. Then they placed a large stone over the opening to the tomb.

Tell the children that Jesus was willing to die for us because He loves us. When we try hard not to make wrong choices, we are showing Jesus how much we love Him.

Living the Lesson

Take the children to church and show them the Stations of the Cross. Let them walk slowly and look at each Station. Remind them what each Station represents. Say a short prayer with them before leaving church.

Extending the Lesson

Art and Craft Project

Materials Needed

"Stations of the Cross" pages (73–79) from the Kindergarten Workbook; a stapler.

Remove the pages of the "Stations of the Cross" from the Workbook. Have the children assemble the pages in the correct order, and staple the pages together to make a booklet. Encourage the children to use the booklet during Lent to pray the Stations of the Cross.

Worksheets

The worksheets can be sent home to be completed or can be completed in the classroom and then sent home. In either case, the worksheets should be used as take-home material because they furnish the basis for parent–child faith discussions at home.

Kindergarten. Worksheets 73–79 can be used (1) as suggested in the Application portion of the Lesson Presentation; or (2) after the Living the Lesson section; or (3) as suggested in the Art and Craft Project.

Lesson 26 Palm Sunday

Workbook Pages
Pre-school A. 48
Pre-school B. 99
Kindergarten 80

Lesson Focus

Palm Sunday is the beginning of Holy Week. On the first Palm Sunday, Jesus entered Jerusalem amid the cheers and the praises of the people, a definite contrast to what would happen to Him at the end of this Holy Week!

The vocabulary word is **Hosanna.** Tell the children that the people were so excited to see Jesus, they shouted "Hosanna", which means "praise to the Lord".

Concepts of Faith

What happened on Palm Sunday?
Jesus entered Jerusalem amid shouts of praise.

Lesson Presentation

Tell the children that one day Jesus decided to go to a city called Jerusalem. He wanted to visit the people who loved Him and believed in what He taught. Someone gave Jesus a donkey to ride into the city. A large crowd of people gathered to welcome Jesus. To show how much the people loved Jesus, they waved palm branches they cut from trees. Some people even put their coats on the ground so Jesus could ride over them. They followed Jesus all the way into Jerusalem. It was like a big parade! As Jesus went by, the people shouted, "Hosanna", which is like saying "praise to the Lord". All were excited to see Jesus, and they praised Him.

Living the Lesson

1. Show the children a piece of a palm branch similar to those their parents will receive in church. Tell the children the palm branch is not something to be played with. It has been blessed by the priest. The palm branch helps us remember we should praise Jesus often.
2. **How do we praise Jesus?** (By saying prayers, by going to Mass, by thanking Him for all He has given us, by always trying to act as images of God, and so forth.)

Extending the Lesson

Art and Craft Projects

Materials Needed

    A. Green construction paper, scissors.

    B. Donkey puppet pattern, gray and red construction paper, brown lunch bags, scissors, glue.

    A. Palm Branches. Cut a "palm branch" from green construction paper for each child. Tell the Palm Sunday story again. Have the children wave their palms and say "Hosanna" along with the story.

    B. Donkey Puppet. Cut out the pieces for the puppet (pattern provided) from construction paper for each child. Pieces A, B, and D should be cut from gray construction paper. Piece C may be cut from red paper. Laying each lunch bag flat, glue piece A (the face) to the flap on the bottom of the bag. Glue piece B (the upper jaw) under the flap. Glue piece C (the lower jaw) below the flap, under piece B. Glue two pieces cut from D (ears) to the top of the head. Have the children put their hands in the bags to make their puppets work. Tell the children that Jesus rode a donkey into Jerusalem.

Use this pattern from the special pattern packet.

B.

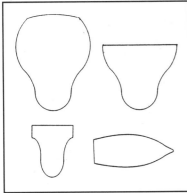

Action Rhyme

> Jesus rode a donkey (*Riding action.*)
> Through the streets of town.
> The people said "Hosanna" (*Pretend to wave branches*)
> And laid palm branches down. (*Bend to floor.*)

Prayer

> *Dear Jesus, we praise and thank You for all You have given us. Glory and praise to You, Lord Jesus. Amen.*

Worksheets

The worksheets can be sent home to be completed or can be completed in the classroom and then sent home. In either case, the worksheets should be used as take-home material because they furnish the basis for parent–child faith discussions at home.

    Pre-school A. Worksheet 48 relates to the lesson theme and can be distributed to the children after the Application portion of the Lesson Presentation to reinforce the concept.

    Pre-school B. Worksheet 99 relates to the lesson theme and can be distributed to the children after the Application portion of the Lesson Presentation to reinforce the concept.

    Kindergarten. Worksheet 80 relates to the lesson theme and can be distributed to the children after the Application portion of the Lesson Presentation to reinforce the concept.

Lesson 27   Holy Week

Workbook Pages
Pre-school A. 49–50
Pre-school B. 100
Kindergarten 81–82

Lesson Focus

The condemnation and execution of Jesus were horrible evils, and yet from the Cross, from His death, came the most wonderful good the human race has ever known: the restoration of grace. On the Cross, God loves us in a merciful way. He draws good from evil. Jesus draws the good of our redemption from the evil of His terrible death on the Cross. As images of God, we are invited to do exactly what Jesus did. From the evil of our suffering we are to draw good. When united in love to the sufferings of Jesus, our sufferings are redemptive. Thus the Cross is a school of love, and we are able to learn from it.

Holy Week includes: Palm Sunday, the day people sang "Hosanna" to Jesus; Holy Thursday, the day of the Last Supper; Good Friday, the day Jesus died; Holy Saturday, the day Jesus' body lay in the tomb.

Concepts of Faith

What happened on Holy Thursday?
On Holy Thursday, Jesus and the Apostles shared the Last Supper, the first Mass.

What happened on Good Friday?
On Good Friday, Jesus died on the Cross.

Lesson Presentation

Application

Holy Thursday
Explain to the children that Jesus knew that He would soon die. He wanted to have one last important meal with His friends, the Apostles. We call this important meal the Last Supper. Show the children a picture of the Last Supper. Remind them of the names of the Apostles (see list in Lesson 13, pages 96–97).

At the Last Supper, Jesus took bread and wine and changed them into His Body and Blood. He gave the Apostles the gift of offering Mass. Holy Thursday is an important night for us as Catholics. Jesus offered the first Mass, and He made His friends, the Apostles, the first priests.

Good Friday
Tell the children that there were some men who did not like Jesus. They did not believe what Jesus taught. These men did not like it when all the people cheered for Jesus. They wanted to hurt Jesus so that the people would stop believing in Him. On Holy Thursday night, these men came with a group of people. They took Jesus

away. When this happened, Jesus' special friends, the Apostles, were afraid. The men who did not like Jesus tied Him up and hurt Him. The next day, Friday, they made a cross out of wood and gave it to Jesus to carry. Finally they nailed Jesus to the cross, and He died.

We call the day Jesus died Good Friday. Jesus died on the Cross to show us how much He loves us. Even though it was very wrong for those people to hurt Jesus, a great good came from it. By dying, He gave us the gift of God's life. With this gift we can share God's life now, and we can live with God in heaven someday. This gift also helps us be the best images of God we can be.

Living the Lesson

1. **Whom did Jesus eat with on Holy Thursday?** (His friends, the Apostles.)
2. **What is this important meal called?** (The Last Supper.)
3. **What happened at the Last Supper?** (Jesus changed bread and wine into His Body and Blood and made the Apostles the first priests.)
4. **What happened on Good Friday?** (Jesus died on the Cross.)
5. **Why do we call it "Good" Friday?** (Because by dying Jesus gave us a great good—the gift of God's own life, a life we can share now. With this gift of God's life, we can also live with God in heaven someday.)

Prayer

Thank You, Jesus, for loving us so much that You died on the Cross for us. Amen.

Worksheets

The worksheets can be sent home to be completed or can be completed in the classroom and then sent home. In either case, the worksheets should be used as take-home material because they furnish the basis for parent–child faith discussion at home.

Pre-school A. Worksheets 49 and 50 relate to the lesson theme and can be distributed to the children after the Application portion of the Lesson Presentation to reinforce the concept.

Pre-school B. Worksheet 100 relates to the lesson theme and can be distributed to the children after the Application portion of the Lesson Presentation to reinforce the concept.

Kindergarten. Worksheet 81 relates to the lesson theme and can be distributed to the children after the Application portion of the Lesson Presentation to reinforce the concept. Worksheet 82 can be distributed to the children after the Living the Lesson section to help the children relate the theme to their daily lives.

Lesson 28   Easter Sunday

Workbook Pages
Pre-school A. 51–52
Pre-school B. 101–102
Kindergarten 83

Lesson Focus

Easter is the celebration of new life. At this time we remember Jesus' triumph over death, His Resurrection. Easter is the most joyous feast of the Church, celebrating the "new life" we received from Jesus.

Explain to the children that we are happy that Jesus rose from the dead on Easter. We know He is with us now and always. He is our King, and His Kingdom is both here on earth and in heaven. We want to live with Jesus now, and we hope to be with Him someday in heaven.

Concepts of Faith

What happened on Easter Sunday?
On Easter Sunday, Jesus rose from the dead.

Lesson Presentation

Application

Review the presentation of the lessons on Palm Sunday (26) and Holy Week (27). Tell the children that after the Apostles put Jesus in His grave on Good Friday, a large stone was rolled in front of the tomb. The soldiers rolled the stone into place so that no one would be able to see Jesus. They even put a guard by the stone. The Apostles and Jesus' other friends were very sad and upset. They all went to one house and stayed together. On Sunday morning, some of the women who were friends of Jesus decided they wanted to bring flowers to Jesus' grave. They hurried to the grave. When they got there, they found the guard lying on the ground and the big stone moved away. They looked in the grave. They saw a wonderful sight! Two angels were there. They said to the women, "Why do you look for Jesus in a grave? He is not here."

The women were so excited they ran back to the house to tell the Apostles. The Apostles were all very excited to hear their news.

Later, Jesus talked with His friends and told Him He was alive. His friends were very happy! They went out and started telling more people about Jesus and His great love.

Living the Lesson

The people who loved Jesus praised Him. We praise Him now, too, because He is with us forever.

1. **How did the people feel when they saw Jesus in Jerusalem?** (They were happy and excited to see Him.)
2. **What was Jesus riding on?** (A donkey.)

3. **What did the people wave?** (Palm branches.)
4. **What did the people shout out?** ("Hosanna".)
5. **Did all the people love and believe in Jesus?** (No.)
6. **What did the people who did not like Jesus make Him carry?** (A wooden cross.)
7. **What happened on Good Friday?** (Jesus died on the Cross.)
8. **What happened in three days?** (Jesus rose from the dead.)
9. **Is Jesus with us today?** (Yes, in a special way.)

Extending the Lesson

Art and Craft Project

Materials Needed

White construction paper, yellow pipe cleaners, scissors, lily pattern, glue or tape, green paper.

Easter Lily. Using the pattern provided, cut a lily from white construction paper. Form the paper into the shape of a cone. Secure it with glue or tape. Place yellow pipe cleaners through the cone, securing them with glue or tape to keep them from falling out. Curl the tops of the pipe cleaners. Cut a stem and leaves out of green paper and attach them with glue or tape. The children could take their Easter "lilies" home as gifts for their parents.

Prayer

> Dear Jesus, thank You for the gift of Your Life.
> You died on the Cross for us.
> You are risen. Alleluia.
> Amen.

Worksheets

The worksheets can be sent home to be completed or can be completed in the classroom and then sent home. In either case, the worksheets should be used as take-home material because they furnish the basis for parent–child faith discussion at home.

Pre-school A. Worksheet 51 relates to the lesson theme and can be distributed to the children after the Application portion of the Lesson Presentation, to reinforce the concept. Worksheet 52 can be distributed after the Living the Lesson section to help the children relate the theme to their daily lives.

Pre-school B. Worksheet 101 can be distributed after the Living the Lesson section to help the children relate the theme to their daily lives. Worksheet 102 relates to the lesson theme and can be distributed to the children after the Application portion of the Lesson Presentation to reinforce the concept.

Kindergarten. Worksheet 83 relates to the lesson theme and can be distributed to the children after the Application portion of the Lesson Presentation to reinforce the concept, or after the Living the Lesson section to help the children relate the theme to their daily lives.

Use this pattern from the special pattern packet.

A.

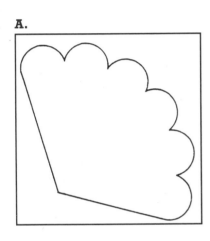

Resources

Daughters of St. Paul, *Fifty-Seven Saints for Boys and Girls* (Boston: St. Paul Editions, 1980).

Hanley, Boniface, *Ten Christians* (Notre Dame, Ind.: Ave Maria Press, 1979).

Hogan, Richard M., *The Wonder of Human Sexuality* (St. Paul, Minn.: Leaflet Missal, 1985).

Hogan, Richard M., and John M. LeVoir, *Covenant of Love* (New York: Doubleday, 1985).

Kelly, Bennet, *The New St. Joseph First Communion Catechism*, rev. ed. (New York: Catholic Book Co., 1963).

Lee, Frank, *Bedtime Stories of the Saints, Book One* and *Book Two* (Liguori, Mo.: Liguori Publications, 1980).

Lovasik, Lawrence G., *St. Joseph Picture Book Series* (New York: Catholic Book Co., 1978–81).

Teacher's Notes:

Teacher's Notes:

Teacher's Notes:

Teacher's Notes:

Teacher's Notes:

Teacher's Notes:

Teacher's Notes: